The Law, the Sabbath and New Covenant Christianity

Christian Freedom under the Teaching of Jesus

Anthony F. Buzzard, MA (Oxon.), MA Th.

© Restoration Fellowship, 2005
www.restorationfellowship.org

Atlanta Bible College
800-347-4261

Table of Contents

Introduction 5

The Law, the Sabbath and New Covenant Christianity 11

More on Galatians and the Law 53

More on Colossians 2:16, 17 and the Sabbath Question ... 60

The Sabbath and the Law 70

Christians and the Law (by Charles Hunting) 74

Letter to a Friend 98

Introduction

A central question faces all of us, provided we take time out of our busy lives to ask and ponder it. It is the question of our personal destiny — more precisely, the question about what we must think, believe and do to be acceptable to God, our Creator. The answers to this question in our time are as diverse and confusing as the number of divided denominations which characterize what we know as Christianity. The various Christian groups make their contradictory claims to provide a solution to life's puzzle. They propose to tell us what we must do to be saved. But they do not agree.

Denominations are created, not least the vast Protestant movement which arose in opposition to the established Roman Catholic Church in 1517, when someone or a group of Bible students "discover" a better way to approach God and serve Him. Often such movements stem from a new insight, the claim to recover a forgotten truth, the correction of a traditional teaching which is not securely based on Scripture.

Much of the conflict which has arisen in regard to the "correct" understanding of Jesus and the Bible has centered around matters of behavior. What is a Christian to do to be pleasing to God? For a substantial number of believers, the selection of the right day for rest and weekly worship has been a crucial issue. That question about weekly observance is often linked to other matters of "law," for example a decision not to eat certain foods listed as taboo in the Old Testament. The disagreements which follow when some believers conclude that days and foods are of vital importance for Christian performance and salvation have led to the formation of whole denominations, such as the Worldwide Church of God founded by Herbert Armstrong and the Seventh-Day Adventists who look to Ellen White as inspired founder. Once established, the denominational "distinctives" become a matter of deeply embedded conviction and even of party spirit, fostering a "them and us" mentality which easily makes an objective Biblical examination impossible.

But examining the Scriptures for Truth is the essence of good discipleship (Acts 17:11). If truth is to be achieved — the truth which makes us really free — we must be prepared to lay aside long-held convictions which we may have taken on when not adequately equipped to do accurate Bible study. It is an illusion to suppose that with good will and almost no training in reading the Bible, we can arrive at all the right positions on biblical matters of conduct and creed.

Many of us have learned the hard way. Once exposed to the notion that Christianity is primarily a matter of accepting the ten commandments as given to Israel and following them in the letter, we were convinced despite all evidence to the contrary that we had joined "the only true Church." Building our own theological cocoon we were unimpressed when others pointed out that our teachers/leaders had had no formal training in the history of Bible interpretation, little exposure to what others had written on crucial questions, and no knowledge of the original languages of Scripture. Surely, we argued, sincerity was enough to guarantee a sort of infallibility. Our leader really was God's end-time apostolic gift to the world, we argued in our naivety and inexperience. And we were marked out by our faithful resting on Saturday! Only years later did we become wise enough to think that we might have been misled.

The issue we tackle in this book has to do with some aspects of the way to salvation, and particularly the matter of obedience to Jesus, since Jesus said often and emphatically that following him and his teachings is the essence of success before God. The question, however, which needs careful treatment is, What is entailed in obedience?

Even a superficial exposure to the Bible reveals that much is said about believing in relation to behavior. Much of the New Testament is dedicated to defining what God requires, not according to the law of Moses under the Old Covenant, but under the New Covenant taught and ratified by Jesus as the final agent of God, the prophet who was to supersede even Moses (Deut. 18:15-18; John 1:17).

Reflection over many years of teaching and study has brought us to the settled conviction that one of the most fatal misunderstandings of Jesus and the New Covenant occurs when we try to mix two different systems, the Old and the New. God is no longer dealing with mankind in the terms He authorized through Moses. If, with full sincerity and a desire to obey God, we approach Him on a basis which He does *not* prescribe for us under the New Covenant brought by Jesus, we are liable to inflict upon ourselves a terrible theological wound. Ignorance of the New Covenant is as divisive as it is destructive of spirituality. But such misunderstanding often parades as "Christian."

We must gain the freedom which Jesus promised, and it is a freedom based on the spirit of truth and not on our own constructions built on a confusing mixing of two covenants. Moreover, Jesus did not give all of the truth during his historical ministry. He continued to speak through chosen Apostles, as he had promised: "I have many more things to say to you, but you cannot bear them now. But when he, the spirit of truth comes, he will guide you into all the truth, for he will not speak on his own, but whatever he hears he will speak and he will disclose to you what is to come. He will glorify me for he will take of mine and will disclose it to you" (John 16:12-14).

All sorts of abuses can arise when verses of the Bible are pulled out of their context and made to communicate what was intended for one period of time but not necessarily for everyone for all time. The classic example is found in a popular use of Malachi 3:10 to impose a tithing system on the church. However, only a few verses later (4:4) the prophet exhorts his audience to "remember the law of My servant Moses, the decrees and laws which I gave at Horeb for all Israel."

Discernment in regard to God's dealings with mankind under different circumstances is required if we are to determine what God wants of us today. To that question — the content of obedience for us as Christians — we address the following pages, convinced that freedom in Christ is the only successful formula for finding the faith as the New Testament presents it. When the one Church unites in that freedom as exponents of the Gospel of the Kingdom and with the Jew-Gentile barrier broken down, as Christ desired it to be, the faith will be vibrant and effective. As long as misunderstandings over the law and its relationship to the New Covenant divide us, the witness of the body of Christ will continue to be damaged.

Christians recognize Moses as the mediator of the Old Covenant established between the God of Israel and His people. Exodus 24 records the confirmation of the covenant arrangements, when the people agreed to comply with all the words written in the book of the covenant.

Introduction

Blood was then sprinkled on the altar and on the people; the congregation of Israel agreed to do "everything the Lord has said." The blood then officially ratified the covenant on the basis of "all the words" Moses had received from God.

Jesus is introduced in the New Testament as the Messenger of the New Covenant. Jesus is contrasted with Moses. "The law was given by Moses but grace and truth came by Jesus Christ." Matthew records five blocks of Jesus' New Covenant teaching, ending with the repeated phrase "when Jesus had finished saying these things" (7:28, etc.). Jesus then shed his own blood to bring that New Covenant into force.

There are matters of critical importance in this issue of discerning what God requires under the Christian New Covenant. Not to advance from the Old to the New is a very serious danger for believers. The tendency to revert to the Old Covenant and mix it with the New called forth the Apostle's sternest warnings and indignation: "You foolish Galatians! Who has bewitched you? Before your eyes Jesus Christ was clearly portrayed as crucified...Did you receive the spirit by observing the law, or by believing what you heard?...It is for freedom that Christ has set you free. Stand firm, then, and do not let yourselves be burdened again with a yoke of slavery. Mark my words! I, Paul, tell you that if you get circumcised, Christ will be of no value to you at all. Again I declare to every man who lets himself be circumcised that he is obligated to obey the whole law. You who are trying to be justified by law have been alienated from Christ; you have fallen from grace...The only thing that counts is faith expressing itself through love" (Gal. 3:1, 2; 5:1-6).

Truth indeed makes us free, but freedom is attainable only when we discover what that liberating truth is. This means paying careful attention to the Gospel/words of Jesus and of Paul, the intrepid exponent of Jesus' Great Commission to preach the one Gospel of the Kingdom to all nations, and who desired passionately that Jews and Gentiles form one harmonious church based on the freedom of the New Covenant.

We invite readers to accept the challenge of rethinking, if necessary, what it means in terms of lifestyle and belief to serve the Lord Jesus Messiah, the bearer of the New Covenant. We have dealt in more detail with the wider issue of the Gospel of the Kingdom in our books *The Coming Kingdom of the Messiah: A Solution to the Riddle of the New Testament* and *Our Fathers Who Aren't in Heaven: The Forgotten Christianity of Jesus the Jew*, and in our free monthly magazine since 1998, found at our website www.restorationfellowship.org.

The Law, the Sabbath and New Covenant Christianity

Some two million believers express their devotion to God by taking seriously their commitment to strict, literal obedience to all of the "Ten Commandments." The fourth commandment is of special importance to them. They see it as a distinctive test of obedience. There are many more millions who claim also to be in submission to the commandments of God, but they disagree with their fellow students of the Bible about just what obedience to God's commandments means today.

Many in the professing Christian world believe the ten commandments are as much the law for Christians as they were the law for Israel as given by Moses at Sinai. This point of view appears to have plain scriptural support. Did not Jesus instruct the young man to "keep the commandments"? (Matt. 19:17). And did not Paul equally stress the need for obedience? Jesus made it clear beyond all doubt that he "did not come to destroy the law or the prophets but to fulfill them" (Matt. 5:17). The natural conclusion from this statement would be that Old Testament law remains as the absolute standard of Christian behavior.

All will agree that no law of God can be laid aside as irrelevant. None of God's revelation is meaningless. Paul understood this well when he stated that faith in Christ, far from destroying the law, confirms it: "Do we then nullify the law through faith? May it never be! On the contrary, we establish the law" (Rom. 3:31).

A major disagreement has arisen amongst believers as to how to apply one particular commandment of the law: the fourth of the "Ten Commandments," which has to do with the observance of the Sabbath. For one camp there is really nothing to discuss. The Sabbath is binding on us as believers in Christ exactly as it was binding on Israel in the Old Testament. Since it was a sign of Israel's allegiance to God, the Sabbath must surely be equally a sign identifying true Christian believers. How can any one of the "Ten Commandments" be modified in any way? To disobey one would be to disobey them all. On this argument the Sabbath becomes the one critical issue which decides whether we belong to Christ or the Devil. Any theology proceeding from a non-Sabbath-keeper will then be suspect because such a person is disobedient to God at a crucial test point. This writer is familiar with this sort of argument, having earlier observed Saturday as the Sabbath for many years. He has since observed, however, that Sabbath-keeping is no guarantee of soundness when it comes to other questions of biblical interpretation.

The Origin of Sabbath Observance

Does the observance of the Saturday Sabbath represent the ultimate in God's will for His people today? Much has been written on the important subject of the function of Old Testament law in the New Testament. Despite the nervousness of many Sabbath-keepers, those who do not rest on the weekly Sabbath are not of the opinion that Christians can disobey God with impunity. The vital question is: *What does obedience mean in the New Testament under the New Covenant?*

A primary difficulty for adherents to Saturday Sabbath-keeping arises from a misunderstanding of the origin of obligatory Sabbath observance. Based on Genesis

2:2, 3 and Exodus 20:8-11, it is argued that the Sabbath day was instituted at creation as a weekly rest for all mankind from Adam onwards.

This account of the origin of weekly Sabbath-keeping overlooks the following biblical facts:

1. Exodus 16:23: The Sabbath day is revealed *to Israel* by God. The Lord says, "Tomorrow is a Sabbath observance, a holy Sabbath to the Lord." There is no hint here that the seventh-day rest had been in force since creation. God did not say: "Tomorrow is *the* [well-known] Sabbath given to all nations from creation." Indeed Moses adds: "See, the Lord has given *you* [*Israel*] the Sabbath; therefore He gives you bread for two days on the sixth day. Remain every man in his place; let no man go out of his place on the seventh day" (Ex. 16:29). If God gave the Sabbath to Israel in Exodus 16, was He removing it from mankind in general? It is most strange that if Sabbath-keeping was revealed as divine law from creation for every nation God would now specify Israel as the nation obliged to keep the Sabbath.

2. Nehemiah 9:13, 14: The origin of weekly Sabbath observance is not at creation, but at Sinai: "Then You came down on Mount Sinai, and spoke with them from heaven; You gave them just ordinances and true laws, good statutes and commandments. So You *made known to them Your holy Sabbath*, and laid down for them commandments, statutes and law, through Your servant Moses."

3. Nehemiah 10:29-33: The weekly Sabbath is part of God's law given through Moses and *thus part of the whole system of Sabbatical observances revealed at Sinai*:

"[The people] are taking on themselves a curse and an oath to walk in *God's law, which was given through Moses,* God's servant, and to keep and to observe all the commandments of God our Lord, and His ordinances and His statutes...As for the peoples of the land who bring wares or any grain on the Sabbath day to sell, we will not buy from them on *the Sabbath* or *a holy day;* and we will forego the crops the *seventh year*...We also placed ourselves under obligation to contribute yearly one third of a shekel for the service of the house of our God: for the showbread, for the continual grain offering, for the continual burnt offering, *the Sabbaths, the new moon,* for *the appointed times,* for the holy things and for the sin offerings to make atonement for Israel, and all the work of the house of our God."

Notice that Israel was bound to a whole system of Sabbaths and holy days.

4. The purpose of the Sabbath, though it reflects God's rest at creation (Ex. 20:11), is *specifically to commemorate the Exodus of the nation of Israel from Egypt.* That is why the fourth commandment was given: "You shall remember that you were a slave in the land of Egypt, and the Lord your God brought you out of there by a mighty hand and by an outstretched arm; *therefore* the Lord your God commanded you [Israel, not mankind from creation] to observe the Sabbath day" (Deut. 5:15).

5. The covenant made with Israel at Horeb was *not made with the fathers (Abraham, Isaac and Jacob).* The ten commandments cannot therefore represent some universal law given to all mankind. The statement in Deuteronomy 5:3 is specific: "The Lord did *not* make this covenant with our fathers." The Sabbath was given to Israel as a sign of God's special relationship with Israel, "that they might know that I am the Lord who sanctifies them" (Ezek. 20:12). This would have no point if the Sabbath was required of all nations. It is a particular mark of God's dealing with one nation, Israel.

6. The Jews should be credited with some understanding of the origin of their national Sabbath. In Jubilees 2:19-21, 31 we learn that: "the Creator of all things...did not sanctify all peoples and nations to keep Sabbath thereon, but Israel alone."

Confirmation of the biblical texts we have cited above comes from rabbinical literature. *Genesis Rabbah* states that the seventh day of creation was God's Sabbath, but not humanity's. In the Mishnah under *Shabbata,* we find that "if a Gentile comes to put out the fire, they must not say to him, 'do not put it out,' since they [Israel] are not answerable for his keeping the Sabbath." The reason for this is that "the Sabbath is a perpetual covenant between Me and the children of Israel, but not between Me and the nations of the world" *(Melkita, Shabbata,* 1).

From these passages it is clear that the whole system of laws, including the weekly Sabbath, the holy day Sabbath of the seventh *week* (Pentecost), the holy day Sabbath of the seventh *month* (Trumpets), the new moons and the other holy days, the seventh-*year* land Sabbath and the Jubilee after *forty-nine years,* were all part of a Sabbatical system given to Israel through Moses. The weekly rest was a commemoration of Israel's Exodus (Deut. 5:15). Thus Ezekiel states that God "took [Israel] out of the land of Egypt and brought them into the wilderness. I gave them My statutes and informed them of My ordinances, by which, if a man [i.e., an Israelite] observes them, he will live. Also *I gave them My Sabbaths* [plural] to be a sign between Me and them [Israel], that they might know that I am the Lord who sanctifies them...Sanctify My Sabbaths; and they shall be a sign between Me and you, that you may know that I am the Lord your God" (Ezek. 20:10-12, 20).

From this data it could not possibly be deduced that the Sabbatical system was enjoined on mankind from creation onwards. All these passages of Scripture, confirmed by other Jewish writings, point to the Sabbaths as a special sign of God's relationship with one chosen nation.

Since Deuteronomy 5:15 traces the origin of the Sabbath to the Exodus, why does Exodus 20:11 connect it with creation? The answer is that God did indeed rest on the seventh day at creation. However, *the text (Gen. 2:3) does not say that He then commanded Adam and mankind to rest every subsequent seventh day.* If He had said this, the Sabbath could not be a memorial of Israel's Exodus (Deut. 5:15). The fact is that many misread the text in Genesis 2:3 to mean that God rested on the seventh day and blessed every following seventh day from then on, commanding mankind to rest on that day. Actually it was only God who rested at creation and only on the one seventh day which ended His creation. It was not until thousands of years later that He used His own seventh-day rest at creation as a model to introduce the every seventh-day Sabbath given to Israel. God alone rested on the first seventh day and much later revealed the seventh day to Israel as a permanent Sabbath observance (Ex. 16). The weekly Sabbath appears in the ten commandments, which summarized the law given through Moses to Israel, *but it is not to be separated from the whole system of Sabbatical rest given to Israel, weekly, monthly, yearly, seven-yearly and at the Jubilee.*

Claus Westermann, in his commentary on Genesis 1-11, sums up his findings about the origin of the Sabbath: "Indeed one cannot find [in Gen. 2:2, 3] an institution, and not even a preparation for the Sabbath, but rather the later foundation of the Sabbath is reflected in these sentences" (p. 237).

The Ten Commandments

It is interesting to note the Jewish translation of Deuteronomy 5:22.[1] The direct announcement of the commandments from Sinai "went on no more." It wasn't (as other versions imply) that God added no more words, thus making the ten commandments a unique set of laws distinct from the rest of the law, but that the people, as the story goes on to say (Deut. 5:22-28), could not bear to hear God's voice. In response God continued with the announcement of the law through Moses. In this case the ten commandments are separated from the rest of the law because God was interrupted by the extreme fear of the people. In the New Testament, laws are quoted without distinction from in and out of the ten commandments (see Matt. 19:18, 19, five from the ten commandments and one not; Mark 10:19, five from the ten commandments, one not). Certainly the "ten words" were unique in the sense that they were spoken from the mountain directly to Israel. It is also true that laws against killing and adultery have permanent validity for all men. But it is nowhere said that all ten (which includes the Sabbath law representing the whole Sabbatical system) are binding on all men at all times. The ten commandments are part of a whole legal system given to Israel.

In II Corinthians 3 Paul deliberately contrasts the provisional nature of the ten commandments as a system of law with the new spirit of the law which characterizes the Christian faith. The old system "came with glory" (v. 7), but that glory is outdone by the new administration of the spirit. The law given at Sinai was written on tablets of stone (a reference to the ten commandments in Ex. 34:28, 29), but the "epistle" written by the spirit of Christ in the heart (v. 3) is far superior. The law was a "custodian" or

---

[1] *Soncino Chumash,* A. Cohen, ed., Soncino Press, 1968, p. 1019.

"tutor" to lead us to Christ (Gal. 3:24). It was enacted 430 years after the covenant made with Abraham (Gal. 3:17). *It was added temporarily, until the seed would come* (Gal. 3:19). Paul did not say that the law given through Moses was "God's eternal law."

"What matters," says Paul, "is not circumcision or uncircumcision but the keeping of God's commandments" (I Cor. 7:19). But his reference is not to the ten commandments. He did not say "*the* commandments of God as given through Moses" but "commandments of God," i.e., divine commands, and these are now summed up as the "law of Christ," not the law of Moses. If we compare other passages where Paul disparages the need for circumcision, we see the contrast he seeks to establish:

"For in Christ Jesus neither circumcision nor uncircumcision means anything [though in the Old Testament it meant everything, see Gen. 17:9-14], but faith working through love" (Gal. 5:6).

"For neither is circumcision anything, nor uncircumcision, but a new creation [is all-important]" (Gal. 6:15).

For some Sabbath-keepers it seems that Paul should have said, "Circumcision is nothing, but Sabbath and holy day observance, on the correct day, is everything."

We need to emphasize the point that in Genesis 17 one could not be a full member of the community of the people of God unless one was circumcised physically. This applied equally to foreigners living with the descendants of Abraham.

The radical difference between mandatory circumcision for everyone and Paul's indifference to circumcision alerts us to the very great differences of practice between the two Testaments and helps us to anticipate "spiritualizing" of the law in other respects, not least in the matter of the observance of the days given to Israel. In Acts 15 a council was held to address the pressing problem raised by some Jewish Christians who were "teaching the brethren that unless you are circumcised according to the custom of Moses, you cannot be saved…Some believers who belonged to the Pharisees rose up and said: 'It is necessary to circumcise them, and *to charge them to keep the law of Moses*'" (Acts 15:1, 5). Peter's response indicates the enormous change of policy directed by God and the Messiah for the international body of Christians: "Now therefore why do you make trial of God by putting a yoke upon the neck of the disciples which neither our fathers nor we have been able to bear? But we believe that we shall be saved by the grace of the Lord Jesus, just as they will" (vv. 10, 11). It would be a direct contradiction of Scripture to say that the Torah in its Mosaic form was an unmixed blessing for Israel! There was much which was intended as a severe discipline and its purpose was to build a barrier between Israel and the nations. Under the New Covenant, as Peter explained, God has now given the holy spirit to Gentiles as well as to Jews, "and He made no distinction between us and them, but cleansed their hearts by faith" (v. 9). It was the intelligent reception of the Gospel of the Kingdom of God which purified the hearts of every one who believed the Gospel as Jesus preached it (Mark 1:14, 15; 4:11, 12; Matt. 13:19; Luke 8:11, 12; John 15:3; Acts 26:18; Rom 10:17; I John 5:20; Isa 53:11).

Jesus and the Law

It is a fundamental mistake to suppose that Jesus merely reinforced the need to observe all the laws given to Israel through Moses. It is, however, true that he specifically denied that he was going to *destroy* the law or the prophets (Matt. 5:17, 18). How then can Jesus have altered the law while not destroying it? The answer is found in his significant statement that he "came not to destroy the law, but to *fulfill* it." What is meant by "fulfilling the law"?

Does "fulfilling the law" simply mean performing it as Moses required? If Jesus demands that we carry out the precepts of the law as given by Moses, *then clearly circumcision in the flesh is still mandatory for all.* We should remember that circumcision in the flesh was a sign of the covenant made with Abraham (*after* he had believed the Gospel, Gal. 3:8; see Rom. 4:9-12) and a mark of the true, obedient Israelite (just as the Sabbath also identified a faithful Israelite).

The law had said quite clearly: "Speak to the sons of Israel, saying, 'When a woman gives birth and bears a male child, then she shall be unclean for seven days...On the eighth day the flesh of his foreskin shall be circumcised'" (Lev. 12:2, 3). Note also the commandment which ensured that "no uncircumcised person may eat [the Passover]. The same law shall apply to the native as to the stranger who sojourns among you" (Ex. 12:48, 49).

In Exodus 4:24-26 God had threatened death to Moses if he did not see that his children were circumcised. This was one of God's most fundamental commandments to Israel. But was it His eternal law, in *that* form, for every human being?

None of us feels the obligation to carry out this part of God's law, though we can find nothing in the recorded teaching of Jesus while he was on earth which would do away with the requirement of physical circumcision. We do not pay the slightest attention to the eighth day of an infant's life as the day on which he should be circumcised according to God's law. Have we then destroyed that law?

In a sense, yes. But in a different sense, no. We understand from the teaching of Paul (though not from the teaching of Jesus when he was on earth) that circumcision is now "in the heart," for "he is a Jew who is one inwardly; and circumcision is that which is of the heart, by the spirit, not by the letter" (Rom. 2:28, 29).

There is surely a vast difference between circumcision in the flesh and circumcision in the spirit. Yet the New Testament sees spiritual, inward circumcision as the proper response to the command that we are to be circumcised. The law has been spiritualized and thus "fulfilled." It has not been destroyed. It has certainly taken a quite different form under the Christian dispensation.

Jesus embarked on just such a spiritualization of the ten commandments *and other laws* (treating them all the same) when in the Sermon on the Mount he announced, "You have heard that the ancients were told, 'You shall not commit murder'...*but I say to you...*" (Matt. 5:21, 22). "You have heard that it was said, 'You shall not commit adultery,' *but I say to you...*" (Matt. 5:27, 28). "Moses permitted you to divorce your wives, but from the beginning it has not been this way. *And I say to you...*" (Matt. 19:8, 9).

By "fulfilling" the law Jesus is altering it — actually changing it — but not destroying it. He is in fact bringing out the real intention of the law, making it more radical, in some cases (divorce) repealing the law of Moses in Deuteronomy 24, stating that this provision was temporary. This is an important fact: Jesus' teaching actually renders Moses' divorce law null and void. He takes us back to an earlier marriage law given by God in Genesis (2:24). Jesus thus appeals to an earlier and more fundamental part of the Torah. He overrides the later concession given by Moses as Torah.

Jesus brought the law to its destined end, the ultimate purpose for which it was originally enacted (Rom. 10:4). In every case we must see what this entails. For example, what of the law of clean and unclean meats? Does Jesus say anything about the meaning of that law for Christians? In character with others of his sayings, Jesus goes to the heart of the problem of uncleanness: "Whatever goes into the man from outside cannot defile him, because it does not go into his heart, but into his stomach, and is eliminated" (Mark 7:18, 19). Then Mark comments: *"Thus Jesus declared all foods clean"* (Mark 7:19, see modern translations).

It appears that at the time Jesus spoke of defilement, his audience did not understand the radical way in which he was altering the practical effects of the law. Peter continued to observe the food laws and protested that he had never eaten anything "common" (*koinos*) or "unclean" (*akathartos*) (Acts 10:14). But later, when Mark wrote his gospel, the lesson was learned: The law of clean and unclean food was no longer in force. Mark had elsewhere (3:30) added his own editorial comment, and he does so in Mark 7:19. Jesus had been referring to this change under the New Covenant. The law's original purpose had been to teach people to be discriminating in matters of good and evil.

Paul and the Law

Paul, the observant Jew, taught this same "fulfillment" of the law of clean and unclean when he wrote: "I know and am convinced in the Lord Jesus [i.e. as a Christian believer] that *nothing is unclean* ['common,' *koinos*] *in itself*; but to him who thinks anything to be unclean, to him it is unclean" (Rom. 14:14). "Do not tear down the work of God for the sake of food. *All things indeed are clean* [*katharos*], but they are evil for the man who eats and gives offense" (Rom. 14:20). A man who writes this way is certainly not concerned with the distinction between clean and unclean meats and fish given in the law (except as these issues might affect an oversensitive, weak conscience, Rom. 14:15). Particularly significant (and contrary to what Herbert Armstrong of the Worldwide Church of God taught) is the fact that Paul uses both *koinos* (Rom. 14:14) = common or unclean by use, and *katharos* (Rom. 14:20) = clean *by nature*. Armstrong had alleged that Paul did not mean to include things which were unclean by nature (*akathartos*, the opposite of *katharos*). However, by saying that all things are *katharos*, he implies that nothing is *akathartos*. Matters of diet cannot therefore be decided merely from the law of clean and unclean given to Israel.

Standard commentaries confirm our point about Romans 14. "Paul's norm [standard] is that no food is unclean of itself, a statement that stands in flat contradiction to the Torah. This fact alone establishes our conclusions...namely that in the new age of the Spirit, God's demands on us are not mediated to us through the stipulations of the law."[2]

"This remarkable statement [Rom. 14:14] undercuts the whole distinction between clean and unclean foods on which Paul, like other observant Jews, had been brought up. Modern readers inevitably think of Mark 7:14-23 and Luke 11:41."[3]

---

[2] D.R. de Lacey, "The Sabbath/Sunday question and the Law in the Pauline Corpus," in D.A. Carson, ed., *From Sabbath to Lord's Day*, Zondervan, 1982, p. 172.

[3] John Ziesler, *Paul's Letter to the Romans*, London: SCM Press, 1989, p. 332.

David Stern in his *Jewish New Testament Commentary* is remarkably frank. Of Romans 14:14 he says that Paul's words are "nevertheless a surprising conclusion for a Jewish scholar who sat at the feet of Rabban Gamali'el to reach; indeed he had to be *persuaded by the Lord Yeshua the Messiah himself,* for the concept of ritual uncleanness pervades not only the Mishna, one of whose six major divisions, *Taharot* ("Ritual Uncleanness") has this [issue of foods] as its central topic, but the Pentateuch itself (especially Lev. 11-17). The Bible does not always explain why some things are pure and others are not. Hygiene is not the issue; for if it were, there would be no reason to exclude Gentiles from the application of these laws. And the rabbis do not speculate much on the reasons."[4] Stern adds that since (in Judaism) the laws of ritual purity apply to Jews only, Paul's statement "that nothing is unclean in itself should suffice to free any Gentile whose conscience still bothers him in regard to such matters." Stern has not noted that Paul is writing as a Christian *Jew*, and it is Paul who makes it clear that the laws of clean and unclean food are no longer valid for *him*, as a *Jewish* believer in the Messiah. Paul does not confine this freedom to Gentile believers only but reckons himself as a formerly observant Jew no longer bound by the food laws. This is a strikingly interesting lesson about the nature of the New Covenant.

The Question of Sabbaths, New Moons and Holy Days

We have seen that Jesus' intention to fulfill the law certainly did not mean that he was simply reinforcing the laws of Moses. The Sermon on the Mount, in that case, would have been entirely unnecessary. "Fulfillment" entailed some radical changes in what it means to be obedient. Jesus is not just a copy of Moses, but he is the

---

[4] Jewish New Testament Publications, 1996, p. 435, emphasis his.

prophet raised up from Israel "like Moses" (Deut. 15:15-19; Acts 3:22; 7:27). It is the words of Jesus and of his emissaries, the Apostles and writers of Scripture, which form the new gold standard for New Covenant faith. The prophet Jesus, "like Moses," was to receive God's final revelation. The promise would be pointless if he was merely to repeat the words of Moses.

It is obvious that Jesus as a circumcised Jew kept the holy days prescribed by the law. He himself was commissioned to go to the lost tribes of Israel and he acted as "a Jew to the Jews." Jesus advised some to tithe on each herb (Matt. 23:23), a practice which few would follow literally today. However, Jesus himself also promised that further guidance into Truth would be given to the Church after his death (John 16:12, 13). The teaching of Jesus did not end at the cross. He continued to instruct the Church through the spirit in his absence. Jesus speaks to us in Paul and the rest of the New Testament.

The issue for us today as Gentile believers is to discover what obligation *we* now have to the special days given to Israel. We have seen already that circumcision in its original form has been abolished; that the law of clean and unclean is irrelevant in its literal sense. What of the Sabbath and holy days?

Colossians 2:16, 17

We should treat as of major importance Paul's only reference to the words "Sabbath" and "holy days" in the whole of his preserved writings. This occurs in Colossians 2:16. In this verse Paul describes the holy days (annual observance), new moons (monthly observance) and Sabbath (weekly observance) as a "shadow." In so doing he reveals the apostolic mind on this crucial issue.

It would seem quite amazing that if Paul felt that Sabbath-keeping was an absolute requirement for salvation he could describe the weekly Sabbath and holy days as a shadow! This could lead to dangerous misunderstanding. Nevertheless the fact is clear beyond all doubt. Paul does indeed call the Sabbath, the holy days and the new moons a shadow. A shadow ceases to be significant when the reality, Christ, appears. Paul uses exactly the same language of shadow and reality that we find in Hebrews 10:1 where the "shadow" sacrifices of the Old Testament are now rendered obsolete by the "body" sacrifice of Christ (Heb. 10:10): "The law having a shadow of the good things to come..." (Heb. 10:1).

Here the law of sacrifices was provisional and rendered unnecessary by the appearance of Christ. But Paul says exactly the same of the observance of special days in Colossians 2:16, 17. The law prescribing the observance of holy days, new moons and Sabbaths foreshadowed the reality of Christ and his Kingdom — the good things coming.

The point about the Sabbath being a shadow is so important (in view of the immense value attached to the Sabbath by some) that we should look again at Colossians 2:16, 17: "[Because Christ has cancelled the certificate of decrees which was against us, v. 14], *therefore let no one act as your judge [take you to task] in regard to food and drink or in regard to a festival, new moon or a Sabbath day — things which are a **shadow of what is to come**, but the substance [anticipated by the shadow] belongs to Christ."*

There it is in black and white. This is the final New Testament information given about Sabbath-keeping. The significance of the Sabbath day for Christians, as well as of the holy days and new moons, is comparable to a shadow. These days no longer have any substance and will not therefore benefit those who try to observe them. (Do Sabbath-keepers in fact keep the Sabbath properly? Do they, for example, obey the Sabbath command by observing the rules for limited travel on Saturday? Acts 1:12.) What counts now is Christ and his commands. He and his new law are the fulfillment of that shadow. In him we should strive for a permanent "Sabbath," every day of the week. No wonder, then, that Matthew includes Jesus' famous saying about coming to him to find *rest* in the same context as a dispute over plucking ears of corn on the Sabbath (Matt. 11:28-12:8).

Matthew also notes that the priests working in the Temple *were not bound by the Sabbath law* (Matt. 12:5). It was not a sin for those priests to break the Sabbath. As Jesus pointed out, he and his followers represent the new spiritual temple (Matt. 12:4, 5) and he is himself the new High Priest. There is more than a hint here that Sabbath-keeping is part of the old order. We may well say that the law, by exempting the priests from the Sabbath commandment when they worked in the Temple, foreshadowed the Christians' freedom from the Sabbath law while they now carry out God's work every day of the week. Just as the Sabbath of the Old Testament was a shadow of Christ (Col. 2:17), so were the sacrifices (Heb. 10:1). And the priests' exemption from Sabbath observance pointed to a time when those who obey God would do so by complying with principles different from those given to Israel.

Attempts by Sabbath-keepers to retranslate Colossians 2:16, 17 are unconvincing. Some maintain that the weekly Sabbath is excluded from Paul's "trio" of observances. Others hold that all three types of observance are meant. They then argue that Paul does not call the days themselves a shadow but things wrongly added to the days. One Sabbath exponent thinks that the Colossians were being urged to offer sacrifices on the special days. But could a Gentile in Colosse offer a sacrifice according to the law? This could only be done in the Temple in Jerusalem.

A plain reading of Colossians 2:16, 17 reveals that Paul lumps together three types of special observances and pronounces them a shadow. This hardly makes Sabbath-keeping *the* issue for salvation as some present it.

It may be that deep down many Sabbatarians feel as one Seventh-Day Adventist who renounced Sabbath-keeping after 28 years. "I have often wished that Colossians 2:16, 17 was not in the Bible, and it troubles my Seventh-Day Adventist friends as much as it did me, say what they will."[5]

Those who wonder about this passage should reflect on the plain words of Dean Alford in his celebrated *Commentary on the Greek Testament*:

"We may observe that if the ordinance of the Sabbath had been, *in any form,* of lasting obligation on the Christian Church it would have been quite impossible for the Apostle to have spoken thus [Col. 2:16, 17]. The fact of an obligatory rest of one day, whether the seventh or the first, would have been directly in the teeth of his assertion here: the holding of such would have been still to retain the shadow, while we possess the substance. And no answer can be given to this by the transparent special pleading, that he was speaking only of that which was

---

[5] Cited by M.S. Logan, *Sabbath Theology: A Reply to Those who Insist that Saturday is the Only True Sabbath,* New York Sabbath Committee, 1913, p. 269.

Jewish in such observances: the whole argument being general and the axiom of verse 17 universally applicable."[6]

I Corinthians 5:7, 8

In another passage (I Cor. 5:7, 8) Paul applies the same "spiritualizing" principle to the annual Passover and Days of Unleavened Bread. "Christ our Passover has been sacrificed." Our Christian Passover is no longer a lamb slain annually but a Savior slain once and for all, with the power to deliver us daily, not once a year. "Let us therefore keep festival, not with old leaven, nor with the leaven of malice and wickedness, but with the unleavened bread of sincerity and truth" (I Cor. 5:8).

We note that the "unleavened bread" which has replaced the literal unleavened bread is the "unleavened bread of sincerity and truth." These are the real spiritual issues, not the matter of cleaning out leaven from our cars and houses for one week in the year. Christians, says Paul, are to be "keeping festival" permanently. The translation in the KJV is misleading, giving the impression that we are to "keep the feast." The comment of the *Cambridge Bible for Schools and Colleges* is appropriate: "Let us *keep festival* [a present progressive tense in Greek], referring to the *perpetual feast* the Christian Church keeps...not *the* feast, as in the KJV, which would imply some particular festival."[7]

The Mosaic system of law as a set of statutes has been replaced by the law of freedom in the spirit, summed up in the one commandment to love our neighbors as ourselves (Gal. 5:14). In contrast, Paul refers to the Sinai covenant, at which time the ten commandments were given, as

---

[6] For more on Col. 2:16, 17, see page 60.
[7] Rev. J.J. Lias, *Commentary on I Corinthians*, Cambridge University Press, 1899, p. 61.

leading to bondage: "The covenant which proceeds from Mount Sinai is bearing children who are slaves" (Gal. 4:24).

In another passage Paul describes the two tablets of stone, which were probably two copies of the ten commandments, as the "ministry of condemnation and death" (II Cor. 3:9, 7). The ten commandments are definitely not God's final word to man. They were a provisional code of law to be replaced by a higher set of commandments today centering on the words of Jesus and the Apostles: We are to pay attention to "the words which were spoken before by the holy prophets, and *the commandment of your Apostles* appointed by the Lord and Savior" (II Pet. 3:2). These New Covenant words are certainly not just a repeat of Moses.

The Old Testament Shadows of the New

Speaking of Old Testament events in the life of Israel, Paul says that "these things were *types* for us" (I Cor. 10:6). "These things happened to them 'typically' and they were written for our instruction" (I Cor. 10:11). We have no difficulty seeing that the Israelites' "baptism" in the cloud and the Red Sea (I Cor. 10:2) was a "type" replaced by Christian baptism in water and spirit. Similarly their obligation to rest on the seventh day typified our rest in Christ (Col. 2:16, 17). The seventh-day Sabbath was a shadow of an ongoing Christian rest. The writer to the Hebrews passes over the weekly Sabbath observed by Israel and sees the seventh-day rest of God at creation as a "type" or shadow of our "rest" from sin now and our final rest in the coming Kingdom. That "sabbatism" (not Sabbath day) remains for the people of God (Heb. 4:9). The Old Testament Sabbath day has passed away as a shadow of better things now come (Col. 2:16, 17), since

The Law, the Sabbath and New Covenant Christianity

Christ has come. The true light of the Genesis creation is found in the face of Jesus Christ who represents the New Creation: "For God who said, 'Light shall shine out of darkness' [Gen. 1:3] is the One who has shone in our hearts to give the light of the knowledge of the glory of God in the face of Christ" (II Cor. 4:6).

For long-standing Sabbath-keepers a necessary "paradigm shift" will involve some serious study and meditation on the theme of the shadow and body contrast of Colossians 2:16, 17 and Hebrews 10:1, freedom from the law of Moses, the "fulfillment" of the law introduced by Jesus, and the "spiritualizing" of Old Testament shadows taught by Paul as Jesus' agent to the churches. Colossians 2:16, 17 should be read prayerfully and with full attention to each word, and no attempt should be made to avoid what Paul says: The Sabbath and holy days and new moons are a shadow. All three are a single shadow. As such they are hardly a matter of life and death to believers.

Jesus, speaking to fellow countrymen before his death which inaugurated the New Covenant, can still refer to some of the ten commandments (the fourth is never cited) as a beginning point for faith, though it must be remembered that to his inner circle of disciples he goes beyond the letter of the law of the ten commandments (Matt. 5-7). Jesus also told some to offer sacrifices according to the law of Moses (Mark 1:44), but no one now would feel bound to follow that instruction. When Jesus told the Pharisees to tithe on separate herbs he was speaking to men still under the law (Matt. 23:23). To the Christians he spoke through his Apostles, declaring that the whole Sabbatical system (of which one part, the weekly Sabbath, appeared in the ten commandments) was a "sketch" or shadow of the present reality of Christ (Col. 2:16, 17).

It was at the cross that this New Covenant was inaugurated. At that time, all of the New Covenant words of Jesus, given as Matthew arranges them in five blocks of teaching (reminiscent of the OT law), were ratified. Just as Moses had given the words of the Old Covenant and then solemnized the covenant with blood (Ex. 24), so Jesus follows this pattern for the New Covenant.

Until the time of the cross Jesus' followers continued to observe the Sabbath (Luke 23:56) and no doubt circumcise their children. The situation is very different when Paul writes to the Colossians to warn them against enforced Sabbath observance (Col. 2:16, 17). For Paul the ten commandments are now summarized in the higher law of love in the spirit (Rom. 13:9, 10).

Let every man be persuaded in his own heart after careful study (Rom. 14:5), but let us not refuse the plain words of Colossians 2:16, 17 describing the status of the Sabbath and holy days as a single shadow. Should we insist on the weekly Sabbath, we must, to be consistent, insist also on the holy days *and the new moons.* They stand or fall together as part of the whole Sabbatical system given to Israel under the Old Covenant.

Attempts to retranslate Colossians 2:16, 17 are unsuccessful — for example the proposal that Paul wishes the "body of Christ," the Church, to judge in the matter of days. This is a forced and unnatural translation. Paul's words are: don't let *anyone,* in or out of the Church, take you to task on the issue of food and drink or annual, monthly and weekly observances.

It is misleading to maintain with the *Plain Truth*[8] that the annual Sabbaths are binding because they were

---

[8] Sept. 1991, p. 18.

instituted "forever" (Lev. 23:41, "a perpetual statute throughout your generations"). Only a verse earlier Israel was given an equally perpetual statute about not eating bread or roasted grain or new growth before offering the wavesheaf. Does anyone consider this to be binding today? What about the "perpetual statute" that those who come in contact with a dead person are to be unclean for seven days? (Num. 19:14-21).

Throughout the book of John the feasts are described as Jewish — John 7:2 (Tabernacles), 6:4 (Passover), 5:1 (Passover). The preparation day for the Sabbath is called "the *Jewish* day of preparation" (19:42). John thinks of the Sabbath as Jewish with a Jewish preparation day preceding it. These terms are scarcely compatible with the conviction that the Old Testament observances are now binding on the Christian community. With Paul, John sees the days as a shadow of the much greater reality of Christ.

The matter of the observance of days should be settled by each individual as he comes to learn true Christianity. People with scruples about food and days should be treated with patience until we all come to the unity of the spirit (Rom. 14:1-6): "One person regards one day above another, another regards every day alike. Each person must be fully convinced in his own mind" (Rom. 14:5).

Should anyone take it upon himself to interfere with this precious freedom granted to believers, he should consider that Sabbaths, holy days and new moons were Old Testament types of New Covenant realities in Christ. The danger of legalism is that it may promote a self-righteous justification on the basis of strict observance to Old Covenant law. He who receives the sign of the Old Testament Covenant — physical circumcision — is "under obligation to keep the whole law" (Gal. 5:3).

This statement of Paul clearly implies that Christians are not bound by the "whole law." Those who insist on law, in the Old Testament sense as a code of regulations, "have been severed from Christ...You have fallen from grace" (Gal. 5:4). These are Paul's stern warnings to any who impose upon believers legal obligations which Jesus does not require of his followers. It is wise to remember that it was hostile Jews who persecuted Jesus "because he was breaking the Sabbath" (John 5:18). Jesus' claim was that he had been working uninterruptedly with the full authority of his Father (John 5:19). This is not to argue, however, that Jesus, during his ministry on earth, disregarded customary Sabbath observance.

The Sunday Resurrection: An Appropriate Reason for Christian Gathering

The resurrection of Jesus occurred on Sunday, and Sunday, though certainly not a Sabbath in the Old Testament sense, is an appropriate day for a weekly celebration of Christ's rising from the dead. Jesus predicted that he would rise "on the third day." In fact, the New Testament states *eleven* times that the resurrection was on "the third day" (Matt. 16:21; 17:23; 20:19; 27:64; Luke 9:22; 18:33; 24:7, 21, 46; Acts 10:40; I Cor. 15:4).

These references to the "third day" most probably go back to the statement in Hosea 6:2 (cp. I Cor. 15:4) which speaks of Israel being raised up "on the third day." Since Jesus represents Israel as its ideal leader, it would be appropriate for him to fulfill what is predicted of Israel (with a future raising of the nation of Israel still unfulfilled). Similarly, according to Hosea 11:1, Israel, the son of God, was to be called out of Egypt. A fulfillment of this prophecy is found in the life of Jesus, as representative of Israel (see Matt. 2:15). Jesus "recapitulates" the experience of Israel and he models what true Israel (cp. Gal. 6:16, the church) ought to be.

It is strange that students of the Bible, particularly Sabbath-keepers, who want the resurrection to have occurred on Saturday, concentrate all their attention on one reference in Matthew 12:40, where Jesus spoke of being "three days and three nights" in the heart of the earth. As will be shown in a moment, this is a Hebrew idiom familiar to Matthew which need not be taken, as a 20th-century English speaker might understand it, as meaning exactly 72 hours.

It is safer to found doctrines on the predominant evidence, and that evidence points to the resurrection on the third day. What is meant by the third day? In Luke 13:32, Jesus says: "Go and tell that fox, 'Behold, I cast out demons and perform cures *today* and *tomorrow,* and *the third day* I reach my goal.'" This way of reckoning time has its roots in the Hebrew Old Testament: "The Lord also said to Moses, 'Go to the people and consecrate them *today* and *tomorrow,* and let them wash their garments; and let them be ready for *the third day,* for on *the third day* the Lord will come down on Mount Sinai'" (Ex. 19:10, 11). "When I have sounded out my father about this time *tomorrow,* or *the third day...*" (I Sam. 20:12).

This method of calculating time forbids a Wednesday crucifixion and a Saturday resurrection. From Wednesday, Friday would be the third day (today, Wednesday, tomorrow, Thursday, the third day, Friday). But which day does Luke consider to be the third day, i.e., the Resurrection day (Luke 9:22; 18:33; 24:7)? The answer is simple: it is Sunday.

"But on the first day of the week at early dawn they came to the tomb...Two of them were going that very day [i.e., the first day of the week] to a village named

Emmaus" (Luke 24:1, 13). On that same Sunday the disappointed disciples remark that "*today* [Sunday] is *the third day* since these things happened [i.e., the crucifixion, v. 20]" (Luke 24:21). This third day, Sunday, is the day the disciples had expected the Resurrection to happen, based on Jesus' prediction that he would be raised on the third day. Jesus even reminds them of this after his Resurrection: "Then he opened their minds to understand the Scriptures, and he said to them, 'Thus it is written, that the Christ would suffer and rise again from the dead *the third day*'" (Luke 24:45, 46). That third day is the very Sunday on which he appeared to them and the day when they were expecting the Resurrection (Luke 24:21).

It is not hard to calculate that if Sunday is the third day, Friday is the day of the crucifixion. Sunday as the third day from Friday corresponds to Luke's way of reckoning in Luke 13:32 (above): "Today [Friday], tomorrow [Saturday], and the third day [Sunday]."[9]

Luke's account of the crucifixion and subsequent events is crystal clear. In Luke 23:54-24:1 he records that "it was the day of the Preparation [which is the standard Greek term for *Friday*] and the Sabbath was beginning. The women who had come with him from Galilee followed, and saw the tomb, and how his body was laid. Then they returned and prepared spices and ointments. On the Sabbath they rested according to the commandment. But on the first day of the week, at early dawn, they went to the tomb, taking the spices which they had prepared."

---

[9] Some have argued for a Thursday crucifixion, maintaining that Jewish rules governing the observance of the Passover and astronomical data make Thursday, April 6th, AD 30 the most likely date. But Sunday, counting inclusively, is not the third day from Thursday (Luke 24:21). See also the clear sequence in Luke 23:54, 56 and 24:1.

Imagine how extraordinarily confusing Luke would have been if he had intended to say that the crucifixion day was *Wednesday*! What he gives us is a clear sequence, one day following the next. The day of Preparation, followed naturally by the Saturday Sabbath of the ten commandments, followed by the first day of the week. This evidence should not be avoided.

The question as to whether Jesus and the disciples took the Passover or whether Jesus *died* on the Passover day is best resolved by taking as our fixed point the fact that according to Matthew, Mark and Luke Jesus celebrated the Passover, as did the Jews, late on the 14th Nisan. John did not contradict this fact. John agrees that the crucifixion took place on the next day (the 15th Nisan). The crucifixion day (Friday) was the preparation for the important *weekly* Sabbath falling in Passover week. "It was the preparation [Friday], that the bodies should not remain on the cross on the Sabbath day [Saturday], for the day of that Sabbath [Saturday] was a great day" (John 19:31). The meaning is that the *weekly* Sabbath (holy days are not called "Sabbaths" in the NT) was of special importance since it occurred within the Passover week. Note that John said in 19:14, "It was the preparation of the Passover [festival]," not "*for* the Passover [meal]." The Jews refused to go into the Praetorium for fear of becoming defiled because of the following celebration of Passover week, not because of a presumed Passover *meal* that evening (John 18:28). They would have anyway been clean by the end of the day, which suggests that an evening meal is not in John's mind. Again, the Friday of the crucifixion John called "the preparation of the Passover [week]," (19:14) not a preparation for the upcoming Passover meal, which had already taken place on the Thursday evening, as the other three Gospels tell us.[10]

What then of the much quoted "three days and three nights" of Matthew 12:40? Firstly, this is not an exact prediction if one insists on taking the words literally. Jesus was in the grave three nights and three days, in that order, not "three days and three nights." Secondly, it was customary for Jews to reckon any part of three days and nights as complete periods of day and night. Even in the Old Testament we find a passage which does not require a period of three whole days to fulfill a reference to "three days." In Genesis 42:17 Joseph imprisoned his brothers for three days and released them on the third day, before the completion of a full three days. Several passages in Jewish rabbinical literature confirm the idiomatic use of the expression "three days and three nights." Rabbi Eleazar ben Azariah (ca. 100 AD) says that "a day and a night are an 'onah' [a portion of time] and a portion of an 'onah' is as the whole of it."[11]

This important point is confirmed by the *Commentary on the New Testament from the Talmud and Midrash* by Strack and Billerbeck (available only in German). The following is a translation of their remarks on Matthew 12:40 in the light of its Jewish background: "In regard to the reckoning of the three days, we must note that...part of a day was considered to be a whole day. R. Yishmael (ca. 135 AD) treated a part of an 'onah' (in this case 12 hours) as a whole 'onah' (i.e., as a full 12 hours)...*Pesahim* 4a: 'A

---

[10] For further information, the useful "Note 11" on p. 279 of A.T. Robertson's *Harmony of the Gospels* (Harper, 1922) should be consulted.

[11] Jerusalem Talmud: *Shabbath* ix. 3, cp. Babylonian Talmud: *Pesahim* 4a, cited by H.W. Hoehner in *Chronological Aspects of the Life of Christ,* Zondervan, 1977, p. 74.

part of a day counts as a whole day (the same is true of a part of a month or a year).'"[12]

Some have thought that two Sabbath days must have occurred in the crucifixion week. They argue that the women bought spices after a Sabbath (Mark 16:1) and before a Sabbath (Luke 23:56). This detail should not be permitted to overthrow the strong evidence for a Friday crucifixion, the third day before Sunday. It may well be that two groups of women are distinguished in the account (as also after the resurrection — John 20:1; cp. Luke 24:1). In Matthew 27:55, 56 there are "many women," among whom Mary Magdalene, Mary, the mother of James and Joseph, and the mother of the sons of Zebedee are singled out. The larger group is the "many other women" of Mark 15:41. They may have prepared spices before the weekly Sabbath (Luke 23:49, 56), while the group of three waited until after the Sabbath (Mark 16:1); or, alternatively, spices may have been hastily bought before the Sabbath and supplemented by others bought after the Sabbath. Mark 16:9 (as a very early witness to the facts) places the Resurrection on Sunday: "Now after he had risen on the first day of the week, he first appeared to Mary Magdalene."

The Saturday Resurrection theory does not fit the facts of the New Testament. The Sunday Resurrection gives point to a weekly celebration of that great event. This weekly celebration is reflected in the early Christians' meeting on the first day of the week. Thus in Acts 20:7, there is just such a gathering to break bread. The meeting here occurred on Sunday evening. Luke uses Roman reckoning to calculate days. In Acts 4:3 it was evening, but the following morning is "the next day." In Acts 20:7 the believers met on Sunday evening, the evening of the first

---

[12] Munich: Beck, 1926-61.

day of the week, and Paul departed at daybreak (v. 11), which was "the next day" (v. 7). The meeting in Acts 20 would have included a sermon and the Lord's Supper, which was celebrated "when you come together as a church" (I Cor. 11:18), "when you meet together" (v. 20). The expression "breaking the bread" (Acts 20:11) does not indicate just a common meal any more than it does in Acts 2:42, where it is linked to other religious practices, "the Apostles' teaching, fellowship and prayer." Indeed, as Paul said, "the bread which we break [in the Lord's Supper] is a sharing in the body of Christ" (1 Cor. 10:16). This Christian "Communion" *is a "fulfillment" of the Old Covenant practice of "eating the sacrifices"* (I Cor. 10:18-21; Lev. 7:6), which occurred more than just annually. It would be difficult, therefore, to maintain that the New Testament "Communion" or "Lord's Supper" was celebrated only once a year. The Lord's Supper was celebrated "when you come together as a church" (I Cor. 11:18).

The point needs to be emphasized that the Christian "Communion" or "Eucharist" is not an *annual* celebration of the Passover. It reflects, of course, the events of Passover, the blood of the "lamb" Jesus providing an atonement for our sins. But it reminds us, too, of the great event in Exodus 24:7-11 where blood was sprinkled on the people as a sign of initiation into the covenant mediated through Moses. Christians are to participate in the New Covenant mediated by Jesus. The "Communion" represents the New Covenant equivalent of the sacrificial meals of the Old Covenant — the difference being that the bread and wine, representing Jesus' body and blood, now replace the animal sacrifice. These sacrificial meals were not observed once a year. Thus Paul speaks not of an annual celebration of the "Lord's Supper" but one occurring "as often as you drink it," "as often as you eat this bread" (I Cor. 11:25, 26).

The Lord's Supper was instituted at the time of the Jewish Passover, but is itself a *new ordinance* to remind us often of the death of Christ and his risen presence with the believers until he comes again. The Jewish Passover is fulfilled in Christ ("Christ is our Passover," I Cor. 5:7, i.e., permanently, not just once a year). The Lord's Supper is instituted to mark the new events of the New Covenant and is a "fulfillment" of several different Old Testament "shadows." It is also a "preview" of the banquet to be celebrated in the coming Kingdom. The wine symbolizes Jesus' blood shed to ratify the Covenant which grants kingship to believers in Jesus' future world government (Luke 22:20, 28-30; Rev. 5:9, 10).

The Lord's Supper was to be kept "when you come together," "when you come together as a church" (I Cor. 11:17, 18, 20). Paul was intending to visit the Corinthians within a year, yet he found it necessary to deal immediately with the problems of their ongoing weekly celebration of the community meal, which included the drinking of wine as a symbol of the blood of Christ and eating bread to commemorate his death. The entire supper looked forward also to the Messianic banquet to be celebrated at the return of Jesus in glory to establish the Kingdom of God in a renewed earth.

Meeting on Sunday

The notion that Sunday became important to believers only after Constantine declared it an official day in the Roman Empire is untrue to the facts of history. We have very early evidence (other than Acts 20:7; cp. I Cor. 16:2) that Christians met on Sunday for worship. This was not as a practice enjoined by any law, but as appropriate to the great event of the Resurrection. It is apostolic custom, not a transference of the Sabbath to Sunday.

As one historian writes: "The Savior and the Apostles did not make fixed rules as to the observance of days...nor do the Gospels and Apostles threaten us with any penalty, punishment or curse for the neglect of them [fixed days], as the Mosaic law does the Jews...The aim of the Apostles was not to appoint festival days, but to teach a righteous life and piety."[13]

The observance of Sunday as the day of the Resurrection is powerful confirmation of the New Testament evidence. In the early second century Barnabas (15:9) writes: "We keep the eighth day for rejoicing, in the which Jesus also rose from the dead, and having been manifested, ascended into the heavens." He also speaks of the eighth day as "the beginning of another world." This is fully in keeping with Jesus being the firstfruit of the harvest, and we should not forget that the firstfruit was offered on Sunday (Lev. 23:11) as a type of Jesus' Resurrection on that day. According to I Corinthians 15:23 Christ became the firstfruit through his Resurrection. How appropriate that this Resurrection occurred on the day (Sunday) typified by the Old Testament shadow — the Sunday on which the "wavesheaf" was offered. The one Sunday prescribed by the law as a "shadow" or "type" has now been superseded, since Christ's Resurrection has now happened.

Ignatius in the early second century speaks of believers no longer observing Sabbaths but fashioning their lives after the Lord's Day.[14] Justin Martyr (ca. 150 AD)

---

[13] Socrates, *Historia Ecclesiastica,* Vol. 5, 22, cited in the *Dictionary of Christ and the Gospels,* New York: Charles Scribner's Sons, 1917, Vol. I, p. 252.

[14] *Letter to the Magnesians,* section 9.

describes Christian meetings on "the day called Sunday" for the observance of the Lord's Supper by "all who live in cities or in the country."[15]

This early practice does not of course validate everything which was taught by Christians in the centuries after Christ, nor does it mean that there was not a gradual — and early — paganization of the faith, from the second century, culminating in a fuller apostasy under Constantine. But it cannot be said that Constantine is responsible for Sunday observance. Sabbath-keepers should not be shy of examining Luke's reference to a Sunday meeting in Acts 20:7 nor the New Testament practice of saving money for a collection "every Sunday" (I Cor. 16:2). There is no biblical text which reports that the church (as distinct from the synagogue) met on Saturday for worship. Acts 20:7 testifies to a Sunday church meeting, and it is remarkable that Paul was in Troas for seven days, but waited until Sunday before meeting with the believers (Acts 20:6, 7). Why was there no church service on the Sabbath?

I Corinthians 16:2 may well be a reference to a regular first-day meeting. As the NIV Study Bible notes, contributions were "probably collected at the worship service," not at home, as implied by some translations.

Summary

The Sabbatical system was given to Israel under the law. God Himself had rested on the seventh day and it was this "model" which gave a basis for the Sabbath-keeping later ordained for Israel in Exodus 16. It was not that God instituted the Sabbath at creation for all mankind. It was rather that in Exodus 16 He revealed a new institution for Israel and connected this Sabbath with His earlier rest at

---

[15] *Apology 1*, section 67.

creation. Hence Exodus 20:11 reads: "For in six days the Lord made the heavens and the earth...and rested on the seventh day [not at that time called 'the Sabbath']; *consequently now*, [so the Heb. *al chen* = 'therefore' may be rendered] the Lord blessed the Sabbath day and made it holy." Jesus said that the "Sabbath was made for man" (Mark 2:27), but the man in question refers to Israel of whom it was also said that they "rebelled against Me...nor were they careful to observe My ordinances, by which, if *a man* [i.e., an Israelite] observes them, he will live" (Ezek. 20:21). The "man" here refers to Israel to whom God's law was given, not to mankind.

The words of Paul in Colossians 2:16, 17 inform us that the New Testament Sabbath consists of a permanent rest in Christ who is the substance of the Old Covenant shadows found in the holy days, new moons and Sabbaths. The Sabbath-keeping community cannot agree among themselves as to how to explain these verses (Col. 2:16, 17). They avoid the plain meaning.

Some insist (as Ellen G. White, founder of Seventh-Day Adventism did) that Paul must have excluded the weekly Sabbath from this "trio" of observances.[16] Mrs. White's successors, notably Samuele Bacchiocchi, see that Paul lists all types of Sabbath observance. They then claim that Paul has something other than the days themselves in mind. However, they fail to explain why *the holy days and new moons* are not equally binding on Christians. The

---

[16] This trio is found in Ezek. 45:17 ("festivals, new moons, Sabbaths"); Neh. 10:33 ("Sabbaths, new moons, appointed times"); I Chron. 23:31 ("Sabbaths, new moons, holy days"); II Chron. 2:4 ("Sabbaths, new moons and appointed feasts"); II Chron. 8:13 ("Sabbaths, new moons, and the thrice-yearly festivals"); Hosea 2:11 ("festivals, new moons, Sabbaths"); *Col. 2:16* ("*festivals, new moons, Sabbaths*"). See also II Kings 4:23; Ezek. 46:1; Amos 8:5. See further, page 60.

whole system stands or falls together. Bacchiocchi appears to evade the plain sense of Colossians 2:16, 17 by suggesting that Paul is against *ascetic practices* connected with the Sabbath and not the Sabbath itself. But can ascetic practices be "shadows of things to come"? It is the observances which are shadows found in the law (cp. Heb. 10:1). These are now unimportant for Christians. As Paul said in Galatians 3:23: "Before faith came, we were kept in custody under the law, being shut up to the faith which was about to be revealed." He uses the same language when he insists that Sabbaths, new moons and holy days are "shadows of things about to be" (Col. 2:17). Since Christ has come as the substance of those shadows, it is unnecessary for Christians to insist on the shadow. But if they do, consistency demands the observance of the Sabbath, holy days and new moons.

There is a freedom in Christ which Christians can enjoy and pass on to others. A rigid holding on to Old Testament festivals hampers the spirit of Christ and the Gospel. We are no longer under the law (Rom. 6:14). We have been "released from the law" (Rom. 7:6). We have "died to the law through the body of Christ, that [we] might be joined to another, to him who was raised from the dead, in order that we might bear fruit for God" (Rom. 7:4). To those who "desire to be under the law" (Gal. 4:21) we recommend the important words of Paul in Galatians 4:21-31: The Mount Sinai covenant leads to bondage. For the children of the promise there is a new and glorious liberty in Christ. There is a New Covenant in the spirit. The Old Covenant with its legal system has been replaced by something better (Heb. 8:13). We are not "under obligation to observe the whole law" (Gal. 5:3). If we attempt to do so, we "have fallen from grace" (Gal. 5:4). Now that faith has come, we are no longer under the custodianship of the law (Gal. 3:24, 25). Those who insist on the law *in its old form* risk belonging to the covenant from Mount Sinai (Gal. 4:24). Children of the covenant of law cannot be heirs with the sons of the free woman (Gal. 4:30). Those who cling to the Sinai legal system are not good candidates for the Kingdom of God.

Surely it is clear that all types of Old Covenant rest days are no longer binding on those who seek to rest in Christ, ceasing from their own works daily (Heb. 4:9, 10). In the words of a sixteenth-century theologian, the Sabbath means "that I cease from all my evil works all the days of my life, allow the Lord to work in me through his Spirit, and thus begin in this life the eternal Sabbath."[17]

Our purpose has been to suggest that a number of popular misunderstandings underlie the tenacious conviction of many that God's law expects them to cease from labor for a 24-hour period, Friday sunset to Saturday sunset. This doctrine was not learned from the Apostles, who lay no such obligation on any follower of Jesus. Indeed Paul, we believe, would be disturbed that Gentiles in the 21st century still allow themselves to become obligated to Sabbath-keeping as essential for salvation.

If the Gentile Christians had been required at conversion to rest on the Sabbath day, this would have needed specific directions from the Acts 15 council which decided how far a Gentile believer was obligated to follow the practices of Judaism. Sabbath-keeping, according to the apostolic decision, is not a requirement for Gentile believers. We should remember that Gentiles had been permitted to attend at the synagogues of the Jews, but the latter did not instruct them to become Sabbath-keepers. Only those who became full proselytes to Judaism adopted Sabbath observance. The Jews themselves knew that God

---

[17] Zacharias Ursinus in the Heidelberg Catechism, 1563.

had given them the Sabbath and did not expect Sabbath-keeping of other nations. Thus it would have required a special ordinance for Gentiles if Sabbath-keeping were necessary for them as Christians. Paul later confirmed the council's ruling in Romans 14:5 where the observance of days is a matter of conscience. There is no question of obligatory Sabbath-keeping. (The argument that Paul is dealing with special fast days breaks down, because the issue concerning food in verses 1-4 has to do with habitual vegetarianism, not periodic abstinence by fasting. In verse 5 there is a change of subject: One man "regards *every day* alike." This is not true of fasting. Paul did not say, "one man regards *any day* as suitable for fasting." The reference is to the non-observance of certain days.)

Where Did You Learn Sabbath-Keeping?

Many of us who have been Sabbath-keepers learned this practice from those who had been schooled in a particular way of thinking about the law. We were not exposed, however, to the writings of men who have given a lifetime of study to the letters of Paul and may well have caught the spirit of his writings better than the Sabbath-keeping community.

The Dutch theologian, Ridderbos, whom every serious student of Paul should read (*Paul, An Outline of His Theology*), noted that Paul did not consider himself to be "under the law," but "bound by the law of Christ" (I Cor. 9:21): "The law no longer has an unrestricted and undifferentiated validity for the church of Christ. In a certain sense the church can be qualified as 'without the law.' The law of God is not thereby abrogated. This continuing significance of the law can be qualified as 'being bound by the law of Christ.'

"That the law in its particularistic significance as making a division between Jews and Gentiles is no longer in force constitutes the foundation of Paul's apostolate amongst the Gentiles. He speaks of it as 'the law of commandments contained in ordinances' and as 'the middle wall of partition'...[This law] has been pulled down and rendered inoperative (Eph. 2:14ff; cp. Gal. 2:14; 4:10; 5:2ff; 6:12; Col. 2:16ff; 3:11. Also Rom. 2:26ff; 3:30; ch. 4; I Cor. 7:18, 19). This holds above all for circumcision, but in general for 'living like a Jew' (Gal. 2:14), as a description of those regulations which had the effect of maintaining the line of demarcation between Israel and the Gentiles in a ritual-cultic and social respect...*In Colossians 2:16ff, with regard to the keeping of dietary regulations, feasts, new moons or sabbath days, we find the typical expression: 'which are shadows of the things to come, but the body is Christ's'...All these prescriptions are but provisional and unreal, as a shadow exhibits only the dim contours of the body itself.* Herein is the important viewpoint that with Christ's advent the law, also as far as its content is concerned, has been brought under a new norm of judgment and that *failure to appreciate this new situation is a denial of Christ* (Gal. 5:2).

"There can thus be no doubt whatever that the category of the law has not been abrogated with Christ's advent, but rather has been maintained and interpreted in its radical sense ('fulfilled'; Matt. 5:17); on the other hand, that the church no longer has to do with the law in any other way than in Christ and thus is 'within the law of Christ.'"[18]

The observance of the Saturday Sabbath, new moons or holy days can at best be no more than a private act of

---

[18] *Paul, An Outline of His Theology*, London: SPCK, 1977, pp. 284, 285, emphasis added.

devotion based on personal tradition. It cannot claim to attract from God any special approval. Indeed it runs contrary to the express teaching of Paul that freedom of spirit in Christ lifts one above the temporary provisions of the law, which is now summed up as "love in the spirit." The Old Covenant should not be mixed with the New. Nor should it be thought that one forgets that God is the Creator if one fails to rest on Saturday. The *New* Creation in Christ and his Resurrection on Sunday lead appropriately to a weekly memorial of that Resurrection (see Acts 20:7 and commentaries on this passage) in which we hope to participate at Christ's return (I Cor. 15:23). Nor should believers restrict the observance of the Lord's Supper to an annual occasion. Churches founded by Paul did not follow the practice of groups coming under the influence of Herbert Armstrong. Paul's converts observed the Lord's Supper "when they met together as a church" (I Cor. 11:18, 20). Clearly, this was more than once a year.

According to Nehemiah 9:13, 14 and 10:29-33, the Sabbath is part of the law of Moses. The law of Moses is expressly *not* required to be observed for salvation under the terms of the New Covenant inaugurated by the death of Jesus. This was precisely the issue at Antioch and Jerusalem, where believing Pharisees "stood up and said, 'The Gentiles must be circumcised and required to obey the law of Moses'" (Acts 15:1, 5). (This does not concern just the offering of sacrifices, since there was no temple in Antioch.) The attempt to bring believers under the law of Moses is described as a disturbance which troubled the minds of the converts to Christianity (Acts 15:24).

Obeying God and His Son

What then is obedience? It is adherence to the "law of Christ" (I Cor. 9:21), which Paul distinguishes from Old

Covenant law (I Cor. 9:21). Salvation is indeed granted to those who obey the Son (see Heb. 5:9). Sin is not exactly "transgression of the law," (KJV) but as the Greek says "lawlessness." But what is lawlessness? It is a failure to respond in obedience to the law of Christ. His Christian, New Covenant law appears throughout the New Testament in the writings of those who were divinely commissioned to record his teachings and who learned to obey him through the spirit. A continuing, progressive revelation of the law of Christ was given by the risen Jesus to the New Testament Church.

But we should never forget that the teaching and preaching of Jesus in his historical ministry on earth are the rock foundation of the New Covenant. It is utterly false, for example, to maintain that the Gospel of the Kingdom of God which Jesus always preached was in any way suspended after the crucifixion. Paul did not change the foundation of the Gospel, the Kingdom of God. He insisted with all the apostles that the words and teaching of Jesus were the basis of all he taught as the faith (I Tim. 6:3; II John 9; cp. Heb. 2:3). "The words I have spoken to you," Jesus had said, "are spirit and life" (John 6:63).

If Christians who insist on one day above another (Rom. 14:5) were to be equally exercised about obedience to Christ's Great Commandment to "go into all nations and make disciples and teach them everything that I [not Moses] taught you" (Matt. 28:19, 20), the focus of obedience would be truly biblical. What, after all, is the first commandment according to Jesus? He opened his ministry with a direct order to his followers.

It was (and is) to "repent and believe in the Gospel about the Kingdom of God" (Mark 1:14, 15). This is Mark's programmatic summary of all that Jesus stood for. The New Testament is really an expansion of these initial words of Jesus as he announced the saving Gospel of the Kingdom. And a second commandment of Jesus is "likewise": "Leave the dead to bury their dead: but you go and proclaim the Kingdom of God" (Luke 9:60). (Jesus also commanded that we be baptized in water for the remission of sins once we have grasped "the Gospel about the Kingdom of God and the name of Jesus Christ," Acts 8:12; cp. Matt. 28:19; Acts 2:38; 10:48; 22:16.) More time would be available for obedience to these "laws" of Christ if Bible students were to cease wrangling and dividing over exactly what may or may not be done on Saturday or precisely which day a given Old Testament festival should begin.

If Saturday Sabbath-keeping is not required by Jesus, then believers should be most anxious lest they distort the faith and present a false impression of Christianity to those who desire to know what it means to follow Christ. Should we agree that the Sabbath was given to national Israel, its enforcement on Gentiles who are not under law but under grace would seem to be a tragic dividing of the faith and an added confusion in an already fragmented Church.

The seriousness of the issue is this: What image of Christianity are we or our church group presenting to the unconverted world? If adherence to what many see as the Jewish Sabbath is part of what we offer the world as obedience to Jesus, are we perhaps creating an unnecessary barrier, even a stumbling block, between ourselves and the unbelievers? Could Sabbath-keeping be perhaps only a sign of elitism, comforting to those who believe in it, but detrimental to a clear witness to what it means to be a Christian under grace (which certainly does not mean license to do anything we choose)?

All are agreed that obedience to the Word of the Messiah is the essential basis of true faith (Matt. 13:19;

Col. 3:16; Rom. 10:17; John 12:48; II John 7-9; I Tim. 6:3). Sin is the transgression of Messiah's instructions. Sabbaths and holy days are shadows and cannot be compared with rest or "sabbatism" in Christ, cessation from our own works continuously, as Hebrews 4:10 commands. This "sabbatism" (Heb. 4:9) remains for all the people of God who desire to enter ultimate rest in the Kingdom of God. A persistence in legalism, contrary to the express teachings of Paul about freedom from law, will not lead to rest, either now or in the Kingdom. The integrity of the Gospel is at stake in this important issue.[19]

---

[19] For further study we recommend: *From Sabbath to Lord's Day: A Biblical, Historical and Theological Investigation,* D.A. Carson, ed., Zondervan, 1982.

More on Galatians and the Law

The non-Sabbath (Saturday)-keeper is often puzzled by claims that Paul must have believed in and taught the Sabbath and holy days to his Gentile converts. Colossians 2:16, 17 (apart from attempts at retranslation) looks like a plain downgrading of the importance of all the Old Testament sacred days, the *shadows* being replaced by Christ, the reflection contrasted with the thing itself. Paul in fact refers to the whole sabbatical system, "a festival, or a new moon or a Sabbath," as a *single* shadow. "These things," he says, "are *a shadow* of things to come." Paul makes not the slightest distinction among these three types of observance. It would be therefore contrary to the plain words of Paul to say that he is not speaking of the weekly Sabbath, but only of monthly and annual observances. No one could possibly read Paul to mean that "an (annual) festival, new moon and an (annual) festival" comprise a downgraded shadow, but the *weekly* Sabbath is still fully in force. He did not repeat himself by speaking of the same "annual festivals" twice! Paul's statement clearly and obviously embraces all three types of holy day.

Mandatory Sabbath-keeping seems to contradict a whole book — the book of Galatians. The essence of Paul's argument must be grasped by reading the book as a whole. There is no question that the Sinai law-giving (which includes the Decalogue) is here viewed negatively by the Apostle.

Paul is agitated that the Galatians have moved "to another Gospel" (1:6-9). Christ has delivered us out of the present evil system, yet the Galatians want to go back to it.

The threat is from a Jewish quarter (Titus was not compelled to be circumcised, 2:3). The Jewish believers wanted to enslave their fellow Christians (2:4). They were trying to make the Christians Judaize (2:14), that is, to seek salvation in the works of the law. It is plain that Paul sees being under the law as "continuing in all the things written in the book of law" (3:10). The covenant made through Moses is temporary (3:23-29). However, it certainly does not set aside the promises to Abraham.

The whole point of the Christian covenant is that it confirms the Abrahamic promises and makes believers in Messiah heirs to the very promises of the Messiah and the land made to Abraham (3:29).

Some Sabbath-keepers avoid the difficulty of Paul's sweeping statements about the law by suggesting that he is referring to the *sacrificial* law only. But they must first show that it would be possible for a Gentile to offer sacrifices in Galatia! To tell Gentiles they need not offer sacrifices would be irrelevant. The law in question, however, is the law associated with the *Mount Sinai covenant* (4:24) which leads to slavery. This law is described as a "trainer" to bring us to Christ. But now that Christ has come we are no longer under the trainer (3:25). It is to be noticed that the trainer is not the *penalty of the law* but the law itself, the whole Sinai system.

To be under the trainer is to be under the elementary principles of the world, and enslaved to them (4:3). But Christ came to redeem us from this slavery to law (4:5), so that we are no longer under the trainer (3:25). We Jews and Gentiles were enslaved to elementary principles (4:3) and now you Gentiles are wishing to return to elementary principles (under the threat of Judaism from Jewish believers): "You observe days, months, years and seasons" (4:10). "Tell me, you who wish to be under the law, do you not hear what the law says?" (4:21) The Mount Sinai covenant leads to slavery. Don't be entangled with a yoke of slavery (5:1). "If you are circumcised, you must keep the whole law" (5:3). The "wishing to serve the elementary principles" (4:9) is evidently parallel to "wishing to be under the law" (4:21). It is hardly sensible to say that the Judaizers were urging them to come under *the penalty* of the law. They were urging them to come under *the whole Sinai system*. That system is the law "in the letter" and not the New Covenant Christian law in the spirit.

There is a simple pattern of thought here: The service of elementary principles means being under the law, and the service of elementary principles involves the observation of days, etc. How could the observation of pagan days be described as wanting to be "under the law" (4:21), "slavery to Mount Sinai"? The children of the Sinai system are at present enslaved (4:25). The contrast is between two Jerusalems, *not between Jerusalem and Babylon.*

Therefore, says Paul, don't be entangled with the slavery of Mount Sinai. Circumcision will mean the need for obedience to the whole system. Faith and love are all that is required (5:6). Those belonging to this system are the new Israel as opposed to the old Israel (6:16). The Church is the Israel of God as the new international people of faith in the Messiah. Paul blesses them, i.e. those in Galatia and the wider Church, the Israel of God. In I Corinthians 10:18 he distinguished *ethnic* Israel from the spiritual Israel of God (Gal. 6:16) by calling the former "the Israel of the flesh." The international Church however consists of those who are "the true circumcision [i.e. 'Jews'] who worship God in the spirit and glory in Christ Jesus and put no confidence in the flesh" (Phil. 3:3).

It may well be asked why Paul takes such a negative view of the law here, and in Romans a much more positive one. The answer lies in the different circumstances and problems of the believers in Rome and Galatia. In Rome he wrote to Jews and Gentiles. He accommodates both elements by sometimes using the word law in a special sense. The Gentiles, he says, sometimes perform *the law* by nature (Rom. 2:14) though they do not have the law. It is clear that that law did not include Sabbath-keeping. No Gentile is a Sabbath-keeper by nature. Yet the Gentiles are able to show that the law is written on their hearts (Rom. 2:15). The uncircumcision who keep the law *by nature* will judge the circumcised who do not keep it (Rom. 2:27). Paul has here a definition of law which is not the law which includes *Jewish* holidays, as John the Apostle calls them in his gospel (5:1; 6:4; 7:2). In Romans, Paul urges tolerance between those who "observe one day above others to the Lord," and those who do not (Rom. 14:5). The question of meat versus vegetarianism is a separate though related issue (Rom. 14:2). These are matters of conscience. The eating of vegetables is not directly related to the observance of days. Can anyone show that vegetables, as opposed to meat, were eaten on special days?

Some Sabbath-keepers are admirably consistent in insisting that holy days *and new moons* should be observed. It is clear from Colossians 2:16 that days, months and annual festivals have equal status in Paul's mind. All therefore must be observed. Amos 8:5 suggests that all trade and work in the field ought to be discontinued on the new moon, and Isaiah 66:23 implies that the new moon is a day for worship like the Sabbath.

Sabbath-keeping can of course be argued with certainty from the Old Testament. But the observance of days has been "spiritualized" in the New Testament. Everyone admits some spiritualizing in the New Testament. Old Testament circumcision was barely recognizable in its spiritualized New Testament form. Who would immediately discern the link between cutting the foreskin and an attitude of mind? While physical circumcision in Genesis 17 is an absolute requirement for membership in the covenant people, Jews and strangers, it has become a matter of indifference in the New Covenant. That is a huge change.

Matthew hints at the spiritualizing of the Sabbath as he records Jesus saying that the priests could break the Sabbath *and be blameless* (Matt. 12:5-6). The priests who innocently broke the Sabbath, that is, they were not bound by the Sabbath when they worked in the tabernacle or temple, are a "type" of the new priesthood of all believers. David and his colleagues also broke the Old Testament law by eating the showbread. But their conduct was a justifiable "type" of the New Covenant freedom from the law (Matt. 12:4).

Christ had offered "rest" to those who came to him (Matt. 11:28-30). Would not this be a permanent rather than a weekly Sabbath? The distinctive feature of the fourth commandment is that it can only be broken one day a week. All the other commandments are binding every day. Paul points to the spiritualizing of the Passover: the annual days of unleavened bread are now equivalent to the permanent use of the unleavened bread *of sincerity and truth* (I Cor. 5:8). "Sincerity and truth" are required every day of the week. That's what it means to "be keeping the festival" (I Cor. 5:8). The verb here has a present progressive sense: we are to be keeping the feast continuously.

Polycarp was directly instructed by the Apostle John. He died as a martyr at the age of 86. His pupil Irenaeus knows nothing of Sabbath observance. If John had taught Polycarp the Sabbath commandment he failed dismally to impress its importance on his pupil. This would not be a conclusive argument against Sabbath-keeping, but it is hard to see how the book of Galatians is not. If Paul was not trying to show that the Mosaic legal system enacted at Sinai was superseded by a higher form of *law in Christ*, what *was* he trying to show?

It is not unusual for Sabbath-keepers to admit that they do not understand what Paul meant in Colossians 2:16. Various retranslations have been attempted but they destroy the obvious contrast which Paul makes between shadow (Sabbaths) and body (Christ). The book of Galatians must also be explained by Sabbath-keepers in full view of the fact that Paul cannot have been speaking of sacrifices. The Mount Sinai code (Galatians ch. 4) was not primarily to do with sacrifices, nor was offering sacrifices possible for Gentiles in Galatians. Then what law *is* Paul against? Since he obviously did not consider the food laws to be still in force (Rom. 14:20, 14: "all things are clean...nothing is unclean"), isn't it clear that he treats the observance of days in the same way?

It is beyond question that he dismisses the obligation to keep some law. What law is this?

Jesus "has abolished the law of commandments contained in ordinances" (see Eph 2:15). Sabbath-keepers must give a sensible and plausible explanation of this text and the whole book of Galatians, if they are to convince their friends that Sabbath-breaking is tantamount to breaking all the laws of God. Finally, Romans 14:5 must be shown to be consistent with the need for a weekly Sabbath observance as an *essential* part of the faith.

The fact is that Paul is against *law* in an Old Covenant sense as *the source* of our salvation. The source of our salvation is "Jesus Christ faith" — faith in Jesus *and the faith of Jesus*, imitating his example as a bearer of the Gospel of the Kingdom, and obeying his Kingdom Gospel (Mark 1:14, 15; 4:11, 12; Luke 4:43). The essence of New Testament faith is belief in the promises made to Abraham (Rom. 4), as taught by Jesus and the Apostles. The power to follow Jesus' example and to believe as Abraham believed is supplied by the spirit which orientates salvation in a new direction. The fruits of the spirit are derived from believing in the Gospel Message as Jesus preached it, namely the Gospel of the Kingdom (see Matt. 13:19; Luke 8:12). "Faith comes by hearing and hearing by Messiah's message" (Rom. 10:17).

If you are in any doubt about the issue of clean and unclean meats or the Sabbath, please consider carefully the words of Paul in Romans 14:14, 20: "I [Paul, the Jew] know that nothing is unclean in itself, but to him who thinks it is unclean, to him it is unclean...All things are clean." Paul uses the exact opposite of the word found in Leviticus 11 which describes some foods as unclean (*akathartos*). He states that "all things are clean [*katharos*]." Can Paul possibly have been enforcing the food laws of Leviticus 11? It is clear that he is not interested in those Mosaic laws. In Galatians 3:19, 24, 25 he expressly states that the law of Moses "was added until the seed [Christ] came...The law was our custodial supervisor to bring us to Christ...but after faith has come we are no longer under a custodian/law." To insist on the law of Moses under the New Covenant is to contradict Paul and Jesus who inspired him.

More on Colossians 2:16, 17 and the Sabbath Question

A survey of the "explanations" offered by Sabbatarians for Colossians 2:16, 17 reveals that there is not much agreement among them about what Paul intends to teach in this verse, though it is thought to be certain that he cannot be against at least the *weekly* Sabbath. The principal disagreement is in regard to the meaning of "festival, new moon, or Sabbath." One group of Sabbath-keepers (notably Seventh-Day Adventists) has seen that to admit the *weekly* Sabbath into Paul's trio is fatal to Sabbatarianism. They see clearly that whatever is listed here is being downgraded as a shadow in comparison with the "body" which has superseded it. This school of thought must therefore argue that Paul has in mind *only the annual Sabbaths and new moons*. These observances can, it is held, be dispensed with, while the weekly Sabbath remains intact.

This position was maintained with great sincerity by the late F.M. Walker (*God's Watchman and the Hope of Israel*). He sees no difficulty with Paul's having said in effect that no one should judge the church in regard to "*festival*, new moon, or *festival*," thus excluding the *weekly* Sabbath. His colleague Sabbath-keepers (rightly) find this an impossible reading of the verse: "Paul's use of the term 'holy day' already includes yearly ceremonial Sabbaths. To have the word 'Sabbath' refer to annual festivals would be needless repetition."[20] Walker insists on

---

[20] Church of God Seventh Day, *Bible Advocate*, May 1982, p. 13.

excluding the weekly Sabbath from Paul's "trio." He argues that the "trio" has only to do with the *sacrificial system of the Old Testament* and that Paul is not concerned with sacrifices in Colossians 2:16, but only with holy days. The Worldwide Church of God, however, argued strongly that Paul was dealing with sacrifices and not the days themselves! Walker is able to cite passages from the Old Testament in which the sacrifices are connected with the trio of holy days. He does not, however, observe that the "trio" is still the inclusive designation of all the holy days, yearly, monthly and weekly, *whether or not sacrifices are in view*: "I will cause all her mirth to cease, her feast days, her new moons, and her Sabbaths, and all her solemn feasts [appointments]" (Hos. 2:11).

The new moon is associated with the weekly Sabbath: "And he said, 'Why will you go to him today? It is neither new moon nor Sabbath'" (II Kings 4:23).

The school of thought represented by the Church of God (Seventh Day) and recently by the Seventh-Day Adventist, Samuele Bacchiocchi, sees that the "trio" of observances listed by Paul is a standard designation of *all the festival days* (II Chron. 2:4; **31:3**; Neh. 10:33; II Kings 4:23; I Chron. 23:31; Ezek. 45:17; 46:1; Hos. 2:11; Amos 8:5).

To make our point we list below what we think is incontrovertible evidence that all three forms of observance are considered to be a single system:

1 Chronicles 23:31: "and to offer all burnt-offerings unto Jehovah, on the *sabbaths*, on the *new moons*, and on the *set feasts*, in number according to the *ordinance* concerning them, continually before Jehovah" (cp. "he abolished the law of commandments contained in ordinances" Eph. 2:17).

2 Chronicles 2:4: "Behold, I am about to build a house for the name of Jehovah my God, to dedicate it to Him, and to burn before Him incense of sweet spices, and for the continual showbread, and for the burnt-offerings morning and evening, on the *sabbaths*, and on the *new moons*, and on the set *feasts* of Jehovah our God. This is *an ordinance forever to Israel*."

2 Chronicles 8:13: "even as the *duty of every day required*, offering according to the commandment of Moses, on the *sabbaths*, and on the *new moons*, and on the set *feasts*, three times in the year, even in the feast of unleavened bread, and in the feast of weeks, and in the feast of tabernacles."

2 Chronicles 31:3: "He appointed also the king's portion of his substance for the burnt-offerings, namely, for the morning and evening burnt-offerings, and the burnt-offerings for *the sabbaths, and for the new moons, and for the set feasts, as it is written in the law of Jehovah*."

Ezra 3:5: "and afterward the continual burnt-offering, and the offerings of the *new moons*, and of all the *set feasts* of Jehovah that were consecrated, and of every one that willingly offered a freewill-offering unto Jehovah."

Nehemiah 10:33: "for the showbread, and for the continual meal-offering, and for the continual burnt-offering, for the *sabbaths*, for the *new moons*, for the *set feasts*, and for the holy things, and for the sin-offerings to make atonement for Israel, and for all the work of the house of our God."

Isaiah 1:13: "Bring no more vain oblations; incense is an abomination unto me; *new moon and sabbath*, the calling of *assemblies*, — I cannot stand iniquity and the solemn meeting."

Isaiah 1:14: "I hate your *new moons* and your *appointed feasts*; they are a burden to me; I am weary of bearing them."

Ezekiel 45:17: "And it shall be the prince's part to give the burnt-offerings, and the meal-offerings, and the drink-offerings, in *the feasts*, and on the *new moons*, and on the *sabbaths*, in all the *appointed feasts* of the house of Israel: he shall prepare the sin-offering, and the meal-offering, and the burnt-offering, and the peace-offerings, to make atonement for the house of Israel."

Ezekiel 46:3: "And the people of the land shall worship at the door of that gate before Jehovah on the *sabbaths* and on the *new moons*."

Hosea 2:11: "I will also cause all her mirth to cease, her *feasts*, her *new moons*, and her *sabbaths*, and all her solemn assemblies."

The admission that "festival, new moon, and Sabbath" denote all three types of observance created a new problem for Sabbath keepers. The attempts to resolve the difficulty are far from satisfactory, since they involve an interference with the normal laws of language. Paul simply says that the "festival, new moon, and Sabbath" are a (single) shadow, but the "body," by contrast, is of Christ. The same contrast of "shadow" and "body" is illustrated by the book of Hebrews: "For the law having a shadow of good things to come" (the language is almost identical with Col. 2:17) in contrast with "the body of Jesus Christ offered once for all" (Heb. 10:1, 10). Similarly in Hebrews 8:5 the Mosaic system is likened to a "shadow." In neither case will anyone argue that the shadow continues to be valid since Christ has come. Yet in Colossians 2:16, 17 the holy days are a shadow by contrast with Christ, but a shadow, according to Sabbath-keepers, which must still have validity despite the coming of the body, Christ.

The all-important question is, what in Paul's view is designated "shadow"? The answer is straightforward: "festival, new moon, and Sabbath." It is *these* "which are *a* shadow." In other passages we have no difficulty with a relative pronoun. It refers to its antecedent! The "new" explanation of Colossians 2:17 tries to disconnect the relative pronoun "which" from the antecedent "festival, new moon, and Sabbath," making the ascetic practices the shadow of things to come. But where in Scripture are ascetic practices said to be a shadow, much less a shadow of things to come? This exegesis ignores the obvious parallels of Hebrews 10:1 and 8:5. Paul simply did not say the ascetic practices were a "shadow"; he says the "festival, new moon, and Sabbath" are — just as the sacrifices are — a shadow, now meaningless in view of the sacrifice of Christ who has come and died. Christ is the fulfillment of all those Old Testament shadows and types.

The most recent attempt to argue that Paul means the ascetic practices and not the festivals themselves comes from Samuele Bacchiocchi. He goes to considerable lengths to show that Paul views negatively not the Sabbath, but the practices added to it. He quotes a German bishop, Eduard Lohse, to support him. However, when the bishop was sent a copy of Bacchiocchi's arguments, Lohse pointed out that Bacchiocchi had misunderstood him. The bishop was not for one moment suggesting that Paul did not view the festivals negatively. The relative pronoun refers back to the festivals themselves!

Bacchiocchi, himself a Seventh-Day Adventist, has overthrown the traditional Sabbatarian arguments of Ellen G. White and the *Seventh-Day Adventist Commentary*. He agrees with all commentators that Paul in Colossians 2:16 has the *weekly* Sabbath in mind, as well as the new moons and annual holy days. Bacchiocchi is followed by the

Church of God Seventh Day. Having defined the word "shadow" as "a sketch, outline, adumbration," their magazine asks: "What is Paul declaring to be the shadow or outline?" The question is simply answered: "Paul tells us quite plainly: 'festival, new moon and Sabbath.'"[21] The contention that it is the ascetic practices *added* to the holy days is simply an evasion of Paul's statement. It is another form of the old Sabbatarian argument that Paul was against the sacrifices which were being urged on the Colossians. This argument was eventually abandoned when it was realized that a Gentile could not offer a sacrifice. Sacrifices were offered in Jerusalem and not by Gentiles.

There is a much more serious objection to all the Sabbatarian explanations of Colossians 2:16. Sabbath-keepers seem unwilling to face the implications of Paul's mention of "festival, new moon, and Sabbath" as a group of holy days, listed without distinction. If it is to be argued that Paul was warning the Colossians against a perversion of the days and not the days themselves, then the fact must be faced that *all three types of days are equally relevant to Gentile Christians.* The mention of all three forms of observance must, on the Sabbatarian argument, mean that the Colossians were already observing *all three types*, and had therefore been taught to observe them by Paul. Only then could the heretics impose something in addition to the days. They could not impose ascetic practices upon days which the Colossians were not already observing! On this argument therefore, the practice of the apostolic church was to observe all three types of observance. Paul clearly sees them all alike. Weekly Sabbath-keepers must, on their argument, face squarely the possibility that they are in disobedience by failing to observe the annual holy days *and the new moons*. There are some who see the force of

---

[21] *Bible Advocate*, May, 1982, pp. 12, 13.

this point and are now observing (or trying to observe) the new moons and the annual festivals.

Perhaps this will show that the whole attempt to preserve the Sabbath in the light of Colossians 2:16 is fraught with difficulty. It is astonishing that Paul mentions the word "Sabbath" only once in all his epistles, and then only to speak of it as a "shadow." Yet for Sabbatarians the Sabbath is a (sometimes *the*) central question of obedience. The efforts that have been made to "retranslate" Paul are symptomatic of a desire to make him say something he does not say. One argument proposes that Paul wishes "no *man* to judge the church, but that the church (the body of Christ) should do the judging." This contrast has to be invented, for the Greek does not say, "let no man...," but simply "don't let anyone..." The contrast is not between "anyone" and the church but between the shadow and the body, which is Christ. The downgrading of the things designated "shadow" should not be hard to grasp. In verses 22 and 23 we have exactly the same kind of construction: the "which" of verse 22 and the "which things" of verse 23 refer to inconsequential matters which will be of no benefit to the believer. The present tense verb "which are" (v. 17) is, of course, no difficulty here since in Hebrews 10:1 the law "has" ("having," present participle) a shadow of things to come. But no one will argue that the sacrifices are still in force.

There are now amongst Sabbath-keepers four or five contradictory explanations of Colossians 2:16, 17. There are three variant forms of Sabbath observance. Some keep the weekly Sabbath only, some keep the new moons and some the annual Sabbaths. Some insist on all three. Many are in disarray over which dates on the calendar are the right ones for celebrating Passover or Pentecost.

One shrinks from contemplating the chaos that such division would produce if the three "parties" were to go out together to preach the Good News of the Kingdom of God and the things concerning the Name of Jesus Christ (Acts 8:12). Others of the Sabbath-keeping community are insisting that God must only be addressed by a special Hebrew title, and that the phonetic symbol "god" is pagan. Can all this be the fruit of the spirit which leads to unity? (This is not to argue that unity is found in the mainstream churches!)

The real difficulty for Sabbath-keepers is the threat to the law and obedience which they see in anti-Sabbatarianism. What they really mean is the threat to Sabbath-keeping. The flaw in the Sabbatarian thinking is the equation of Paul's term "the law" with the ten commandments of the Old Testament. Such equation is questionable as can be shown easily by reading Romans 2:14, 15: "Whenever the Gentiles, which have not the law [*nomos*], do by nature the things contained in the law...they show the work of the law written in their hearts." Does this law include the observance of the weekly Sabbath, the annual Sabbaths or the new moons? There is a spiritual law detailed by Jesus in the Sermon on the Mount which is not just a repeat of the ten commandments, even though it was Jesus' custom to enter the synagogue on the Sabbath day. The law of circumcision remained in force throughout the ministry of Christ but no one is shocked by its "spiritualizing" as a circumcision of the heart, as Paul taught.

The observance of days likewise becomes a matter of indifference as Paul clearly says in Romans 14:5 where also the question of vegetarianism and the use of wine and meat are dealt with. It is very significant that many Sabbath-keepers are unable to countenance the use of wine as a God-given blessing (in strict moderation, of course). The refusal to drink wine is a form of asceticism imposed on the New Testament faith. Jesus turned many gallons of water into wine (symbolizing the move from the Old Covenant to the New Covenant). Jesus himself is indicted if we declare that alcohol is in itself sinful. He was with equal injustice accused of being a "wine-bibber." It should be obvious that Jesus treated wine as a God-given blessing, used properly.

Sabbath-keepers must consider the possibility that insistence on a special day is of the same order — a regulation imposed on the faith and destructive of our liberty in Christ. Those of us who know life as Sabbath-keepers and without the Sabbath are not aware that we have moved into darkness. Our whole experience with the New Testament documents suggests the opposite. This sort of subjective argument is, of course, not a strong one. However, the New Testament witness in Colossians 2:16 is powerfully against the obligation of Sabbath-keeping. The observation of the fourth commandment will contribute nothing to Christian spirituality. Resting in Christ continuously as our "Sabbath" is far more important for New Testament faith.

The findings of a prominent Sabbath-keeper of 28 years, after an exhaustive search for truth on what the Bible says about mandatory observance of Saturday, are worthy of note: "I, like all seventh-day brethren, firmly believed and have said a thousand times that the seventh-day Sabbath was never associated with new moons and feast days. It is unaccountable to me how I ever could have been so blind...After keeping the Sabbath for 28 years, after having persuaded more than a thousand others to keep it; after having read my Bible through, verse by verse...and having scrutinized, to the very best of my ability, every text and word in the whole Bible having the remotest bearing on the Sabbath question; after having looked up all these, both in the original and in many translations; after having searched in lexicons, concordance, commentaries and dictionaries; after having read armfuls of books on both sides of the question; after having read every line in all the early church fathers upon this point; after having written several works in favor of the seventh day which were satisfactory to my brethren; after having debated the question more than a dozen times, after seeing the fruits of keeping it, and after weighing all the evidence, in the fear of God and of judgment, I am fully settled in my own mind and conscience that the evidence is against the keeping of the seventh day...Trying to put new wine (the Gospel) into old bottles (the institutions of the Old Covenant) spoils both...When I was a firm believer in the seventh day, Colossians 2:14, 16, 17 always bothered me more or less. The plain simple reading of it seemed manifestly to teach the abolition of the Sabbath. I was impressed with the fact that it had to be *explained away*, and that it took a tremendous amount of fine hair-splitting distinctions to do it."[22] The same former Sabbath-keeper observed: "I have often wished that Colossians 2:16, 17 was not in the Bible, and it troubles my Seventh-day Adventist brethren as much as it did me, say what they will."[23]

---

[22] D.M. Canright, "Why I Gave Up the Seventh Day."
[23] Cited in M.S. Logan, *Sabbath Theology,* p. 269.

The Sabbath and the Law

The Old Covenant is distinguished from the New. The Old is on the principle of law and the New is "in Christ." In I Corinthians 9:21, Paul is "within the **law of Christ**" and for him the "keeping of the commandments is everything" (I Cor. 7:19).

The contrast appears:

1) In II Corinthians 3:13-17 the Worldwide Church of God tried to restrict this to the penalty of the law, but the reference is to the two tablets of stone in Exodus 24:12 — the ten commandments. Paul contrasts the Old Testament law unfavorably with the new "law of Christ."

2) In Galatians 5:3 physical circumcision means we will have **"to keep the whole law" (meaning that Christians do not have to keep the whole law)**. As far as "living as a Jew" is concerned (Gal. 2:14) Christians do not need to, so Paul can be **"without law"** to a person who is "without law." A Sabbath-keeper could hardly say he is "without law."

3) There is a law of commandments in ordinances which has been abolished (Eph. 2:15).

4) Galatians 4:21-26 shows that the Old Covenant (Horeb) is causing bondage and is directly opposed to Christ. Paul actually says that if you come under the law, Christ becomes *inoperative in your life* (Gal. 5:4)! No wonder Satan wants people under the law. This will explain, then, the attack by Satan on the church at Colosse. Here Paul is indignant that unneeded rules are being imposed on the church (Col. 2:10-12).

The Sabbath and the Law

Colossians 2:16 shows what the status of the Sabbath is for the Christians. It and the holy days and the new moons are a shadow. This is exactly the same as the status of sacrifices (Heb. 8:5; 10:1). No one proposes that the shadow of sacrifices is still valid now that Christ has come. So the substance of the shadow of physical circumcision is circumcision of the heart and the substance of the shadow of Sabbaths/holy days is rest from our own works in Christ (Heb. 4). Christ is our Sabbath. We rest in him every day. Paul says, "Let us *be keeping* the feast," i.e., all the time. Unleavened bread is now the "unleavened bread of genuineness and truth" (I Cor. 5:8). Paul has thus "spiritualized" the Old Testament observances.

In the Old Testament the Sabbath is revealed to Moses in Exodus 16 for the first time. Note Nehemiah 9:14: "the Sabbath was revealed to the Israelites through Moses." The fact that God hallowed the Sabbath at creation does not in itself prove that He meant it to be kept by Adam. Exodus 20:11 links the sanctification of the Sabbath at creation with its *later* revealing to Moses. God also sanctified the Sabbath as a type of the millennial rest according to Hebrews 4:4-9. **Deuteronomy 5:3 specifically says that the Old Covenant and the Decalogue were *not made with the fathers* but with Israel, and that Sabbath-keeping was a memorial of the slavery in Egypt (Deut. 5:15).**

Romans 14:5 shows that the observance of one day above another is a matter of conscience, and Colossians 2:16 shows that enforced Sabbath-keeping is wrong. If not, then new moons are as binding as the Sabbath and holy days.

All this is not to say that Christians have no law. The law has been "fulfilled" (Matt. 5:17), i.e., its deeper spiritual intent has been revealed and become mandatory for us. It can be kept only through the spirit. The Sabbath is part of a whole round of Sabbaths/holy days/new moons/land Sabbaths/Jubilee which belong to the Old Covenant. The intention of these laws comes into the New Covenant as a spiritual rest in God, now and much more fully in the future Kingdom.

So Herbert Armstrong and others mixed the Old with the New and did the very thing that Paul opposed so violently in Galatians and Colossians. The Protestants understand this well. Herbert Armstrong's insistence on this special requirement, along with tithing, drew people to himself and separated them from everyone else (the Sabbath does that very well). Legalism also separates us from Christ.

Leviticus 24:3 says that the oil was to burn in the tabernacle light as "a statute forever in your generations." This we now understand spiritually as the light of the spirit and the Gospel in Christians. So the Sabbath as a perpetual covenant is spiritualized. The physical nation of Israel becomes the spiritual Israel of the Church in the New Testament (Gal. 6:16; Phil. 3:3). (This is not to deny a collective conversion of the Jews in the future at the Second Coming.)

There is a strong hint of the spiritual nature of the Sabbath in Matthew 12:5. In justifying his behavior on the Sabbath Jesus appeals to the example of the priests who in the Old Testament were exempt from the law of the Sabbath. **Note that they broke the Sabbath — they worked on it — but were innocent**. Isn't this a foreshadowing of the church which breaks the Sabbath and is innocent? The church's Sabbath is something different: the cessation from our own works every day of the week.

The word "Sabbath" does not occur until Exodus 16. God rested on the seventh day, but it does not say that He then commanded every Sabbath from that moment on to be kept. The Sabbath was the covenant sign for Israel and a type of the millennial rest we are to enter later, as well as a type of the cessation from our own sinful works now, every day of the week (Heb. 4). "There remains for the Christians a 'sabbatism,'" not the literal seventh day.

Christians and the Law (Torah)
by Charles Hunting,
former evangelist in the Worldwide Church of God

Bringing the doctrine of the one God to the attention of believers is an essential element in the restoration of biblical faith. I am convinced, however, that we face an equal challenge in the matter of legalism — the confusion of the Old Testament Mosaic system with the freedom of the New Covenant taught by Jesus and Paul. The question is this: Can the current semi-Mosaic systems being offered as New Testament faith be reconciled with the worldwide commission of the Church? Jesus announced the Christian mission in Luke 4:43, 44: "I must proclaim the Gospel of the Kingdom of God to the other towns also, *for that is what I was sent to do*. So he proclaimed the gospel in the synagogues of Judea." The same saving Gospel of the Kingdom was later directed by Jesus to all the nations (Matt. 28:19, 20). The urgency of the task had been underlined by the Messiah, who challenged a half-hearted disciple in Luke 9:60 to "go and announce the Kingdom of God everywhere."

A word about my personal experience. I came out of the Worldwide Church of God (the Armstrong movement) when I found out that top men at headquarters *knew* that Old Testament tithing laws were not incumbent on the New Testament Church. That study then led me to look at the whole subject of legalism. My mind went back to Mr. Rod Meredith's class in the epistles of Paul at Ambassador College. Why was Galatians postponed to the last day of the course, allowing only one hour for the lecture and no discussion? The fact is that under that Armstrong system many of us had unexpressed reservations about Paul's clarion cry for freedom. We simply could not deal with Paul's express language about the cessation, *in some sense*, of the law, or Torah (Gal. 3:21-29). The law had been added under Moses only until the coming of Jesus. Paul could hardly have made things clearer.

I was present when Mr. Armstrong exposed his uneasiness with Galatians. He told an assembly of ministers in the dining hall at Pasadena not to spend their time in the book of Galatians. It took me 15 years even to think of asking why this charter of freedom from Paul's pen presented an apparent threat to us.

I later found that any attempt to reassess the fundamental issue of the Worldwide theology regarding our view of the law was a futile exercise. I turned in my credit cards and left, not because I was ill-treated but because I was strongly suspicious of our unfair treatment of major New Testament themes.

Subsequently I have spent much time investigating this subject from Scripture, creedal statements and commentaries. I have never been in a situation where the Mosaic system of holy days or food laws affected me personally. But there are parts of the world where citizens would be risking life, loss of education, starvation of their children and possibly jail time for attempting to live by the semi-Mosaic system we espoused and imposed.

We had better be very sure of our ground before asking others to risk their lives for refusing to eat pork. Such demands may have been made of Jews under the law of Moses in the time of Antiochus Epiphanes, but did Paul make this demand of his Gentile converts?

The good news of a coming Kingdom, entrance into which required one to keep parts of a Levitical system in a world totally out of sync with it, was not good news at all, but could be a road to unnecessary and burdensome struggle and opposition. Not that adverse conditions induced by faithful obedience make a system wrong. I am simply asking you to consider whether in fact Paul would have in any way endorsed our partial, Mosaic version of the faith.

There are a number of laws taught to Israel in the Mediterranean which are quite awkward for the rest of the world. I will mention only a few. Harvest-related festivals and holy days in the down-under world of Australia and South Africa do not fit at all with the seasons. They are backwards in southern climes. Spring festivals in the fall, Feast of Tabernacles in the spring. Israel's Levitical rites lose their meaning. Surely there is no need to elaborate.

What about the denial of the rather healthy seal meat and whale blubber diets to Eskimos? We have substituted the sugar-loaded, teeth-rotting Western diet, and the results have been disastrous. Are Eskimos bound to come under the food laws of Leviticus 11? And where are the instructions for the irregular sunsets in the extremes of latitudes? The prescribed days are well suited to the Mediterranean world. Even in the UK one may lose one's job for quitting at 4:30 on Friday evening. When I queried a high-ranking Worldwide minister on these and other problems, his reply was "tell those foreigners to move out." Maybe the Eskimo could move his canoe into the Hudson River and spear the mercury-contaminated "levitically clean" fish of that notoriously dirty river?

As for the holy day and Sabbath keepers of Saudi Arabia, their problem would be rather short-lived. They could be subject to the death penalty in parts of the Islamic world. Would the preaching of the Good News to the Muslim world be enhanced by following Moses as well as

Christ? Is God looking for a company of martyrs for the cause of Moses and the Old Covenant? None of these problems arose in Israel, since all the laws governing religion, agriculture, food, vacations, child-rearing, hygiene, education, judicial system, etc., were clearly defined and reasonable. The package was for a total way of life within a chosen nation. It was quite feasible for the family of Israel. But just how practical are those laws for the citizens of other climes in widely dissimilar circumstances?

Just how do we get the message of the Kingdom of God to people who are faced with hostile governments? Does their salvation depend on adherence to the semi-Mosaic system we advocated? Would our three tithes system really enhance the spreading of the gospel in India and other parts of the world where poverty acknowledges no boundaries? Remember, we ministers were not required to pay second or third tithes. "These tithes were *for* us Levites, not from us." What of the man in Malawi who is the only one of thousands known to us who holds down a job? Is he to tithe on the $30 he makes a month teaching school? He is already paying for his bed on a mortgage.

A conference was held to consider what should be required of the Gentiles in reference to the Mosaic system. Acts 15:5 states that "Some of the Pharisaic party who had become believers came forward and declared, 'Those Gentiles must be circumcised and *told to keep the law of Moses.*'"

The whole Mosaic system was waived. James declared the following in verses 28, 29: "It is the decision of the *Holy Spirit*, and our decision, to lay no further burden upon you [Gentiles] beyond these essentials: you are to abstain from meat that has been offered to idols, from blood, from anything that has been strangled, and from fornication. If you keep yourselves free from these things you will be doing well." It was obvious that these prohibitions were partly in deference to Jewish converts. An additional warning to the Gentiles on the endemic problem of fornication was specifically included.

Were the Gentile Christians thus deprived of the blessings of the Mosaic Torah? Hardly. Peter had said to his Jewish Christian opponents: "Why do you put God to the test, putting a yoke on the neck of the disciples which neither our fathers nor we were able to bear?" (Acts 15:10).

Our agility in the WWCG to take these plain statements and obliterate them by obscuring their obvious meaning was marvelous. The standard of conduct for Christian believers given by Jesus in the Sermon on the Mount (Matt. 5, 6, 7) clearly stated the core beliefs for all converts, whether Jew or Gentile.

Jesus had come to fulfill or "fill with full meaning" the whole of the Old Testament (the "Law and the Prophets"). He had not come to reinforce *in the letter* the Old Testament covenant under Moses. If he had, then Paul would be plainly exposed as a false prophet. (This is the view taken by some who accept Jesus but not Paul — without realizing that such is an impossibility.) Certainly the Hebrew Bible has not lost any of its validity, but it is to be understood in the light of the New Covenant. For example, while *physical* circumcision was absolutely required of Jew and Gentile within the covenant (Gen. 17:9-14), Jesus, speaking through Paul, made it clear that circumcision is now to be understood in a non-physical, spiritual sense — of the heart, internally and not externally. That is a major revision of the letter of Old Testament law (Torah).

That brings us to other biblical evidence. Paul says, "Remember then your former condition, Gentiles as you were by birth, and 'the uncircumcised' as you are called by those who call themselves 'the circumcised' because of a physical rite. You were at that time *excluded* from the community of Israel, strangers to God's covenants and the promises that go with them. Yours was a world without hope and without God. Once you were far off, *but now you are in union with Christ Jesus through the shedding of Christ's blood. For he himself is our peace.* Gentiles and Jews, he has made the two one, and in his own body of flesh and blood has broken down the barrier of enmity which separated them; [how?] for *he annulled the law [the Torah] with its rules and regulations,*[24] so as to create out of the two a single new humanity in *himself* [not through Moses or the Levitical priesthood], thereby making peace. This was his purpose, to reconcile the two in a single body to God through the cross, by which he killed the enmity. *So he came and proclaimed the good news*: peace to you who are far off, and peace to those who are near; through him we both alike have access to the Father in the one spirit" (Eph. 2:11-18, REB).

Paul's remarks address our initial question. I have written this out to save you the time of looking it up and will use the REB (Revised English Bible) translation throughout except where noted. Can we ignore the very plain statements in Paul's letter?

The Temple veil was rent and access to God was no longer gained through the Levitical system but through God's resurrected Son and the New Covenant teachings which he ratified with his death. "This cup is the New Covenant sealed by my blood" (Luke 22:20).

---

[24] The Greek says: "the Torah of commandments in dogmas."

Consider the question of being estranged from "God's covenants and the promises that go with them." These covenants and promises had been made to Israel through Abraham, Moses and David. A major component of the Mosaic system was of course the priesthood given to Levi. Hebrews 8:6 is enlightening: "But in fact the ministry which Jesus has been given is superior to theirs [the Levites], for he is the mediator of a better covenant, established on better promises." There are two *different* covenants, two different ministries involved — one instituted by God through Moses and a different one by the same God through Jesus.

The latter says, "The time has arrived; the kingdom of God is at hand. Repent and believe the gospel" (Mark 1:15). The command to believe and obey the Gospel is quite clear, readily understandable, and available to the entire world. It is accessible to all in its simplicity, unhindered by any set of circumstances, legislative, geographic, or otherwise. It is a matter of the mind not a matter of physical ordinances. The rite of circumcision best illustrates the enormous change. Circumcision has not been abolished! But the physical is no longer required. It has given way to the spiritual. We must still all be circumcised in our hearts. "The real Jew is one who is inwardly a Jew, and his circumcision is of the heart, spiritual not literal; he receives his commendation not from men but from God" (Rom. 2:29). Here, one of the lynch pins of the Old Covenant requirements is finished, but it has retained its meaning in a fulfilled sense. The Old Testament was, as in so many other cases, a shadow of the substance of the Christ who has now come. Shadows fail, but the full intention of the command remains.

The Day of Atonement: Legalism or "Illegalism"?

The first covenant commands a yearly fast day as a reminder of sin. It was annual because there was no lasting effect or freedom of conscience, which is a prerequisite for permanent and unhindered access to God. This can be achieved only through the sacrifice of Christ. This spiritual truth is declared by the writer of Hebrews. "The law contains but a shadow of the good things to come, not the true picture" (10:1). The Day of Atonement is certainly "not a true picture" of the atonement we now enjoy on a continuing basis through the Messiah's sacrifice. Hebrews continues: "With the same sacrifices offered year after year for all time, it can never bring the worshipers to perfection...First he says, 'Sacrifices and offerings...you do not desire or delight in,' although the law prescribes them. Then he adds, 'Here I am: I have come to do your will.' *He thus abolishes the former* to establish the latter. And it is by the will of God that we have been consecrated, through the body of Jesus once for all" (10:1-10).

Who, on the basis of this teaching, can maintain that an abolition of Torah, in one sense, has not occurred? Did we not earlier read in Ephesians 2:15 that Jesus "abolished the Torah of commandments in dogmas"? If this is a new concept to you, please give it your serious attention.

I think I am not stepping out of line in wondering if what we do during the Day of Atonement might not be a denial of the effectiveness of Jesus' sacrifice — and not just a harmless vestigial activity? And should this Old Covenant shadow be taught to the whole world as a part of the Kingdom of God message? I think not.

Hebrews 3, while pointing out the faithfulness of Moses in God's household, states of Christ: "he is faithful as a son, over the household. And we are that household, if only we are fearless and keep our hopes high" (3:6). "The 'today' of the next verse signals a fresh moment of history which is always conditioned by our response of obedience or disobedience, of faith or unbelief."[25] It is something for "now" with all its difficulties and something to be perfected in the future.

But what is the subject of this "today"? It is the entrance into God's "rest." This "rest" can be experienced even now by union with the person of Jesus. "But Jesus holds a perpetual priesthood because he remains forever; that is why he is able to save completely those who approach God through him, since he is always alive to plead on their behalf" (Heb. 7:24, 25).

Brushing cupboards and floors bare of leaven, removing the residue from a trip to McDonald's seem a bit short of the mark when we grasp what Christ's sacrifice has *already* done for us: "May the God of peace, who brought back from the dead our Lord Jesus, the great Shepherd of the sheep, through the blood of an eternal covenant, make you perfect in all goodness" (Heb. 13:20, 21). This, and not our domestic cleaning activity, is the real solution when it comes to our sinful nature. It seems to me that Paul would be highly agitated by a return to the shadow now that Christ has appeared as High Priest (Heb. 9:11). "One greater than the temple, and its institutions, remains with us" (Matt. 12:6).

Paul does not treat lightly this issue of mixing two systems and undermining the work of Christ with works which he does not require: "Your self-satisfaction ill becomes you. Have you never heard the saying, 'A little leaven leavens all the dough?' Get rid of the old leaven and then you will be a new batch of unleavened dough. *Indeed you already are*, [why and how?] because Christ

---

[25] William Lane, *Hebrews, Word Biblical Commentary,* Word Books, 1991, p. 90.

our Passover lamb has been sacrificed. Therefore let us be keeping the feast [note the present continuous verb, which does not point to a single annual observance], not with the old leaven of depravity and wickedness but only the unleavened bread which is sincerity and truth" (1 Cor. 5:6-8). Note the spiritualizing of the literal bread.

The question is this: why should we return to Moses and the Levitical system for our instructions when Christ's sacrifice has already paid the price for our sins on a continuing basis and when the New Testament church celebrated the Lord's Supper *not once a year* but "when you meet for this meal" (1 Cor. 11:33)? The celebration was "when you meet together in church," "when you meet as a congregation" (1 Cor. 11:18, 20).

Something seems terribly wrong with our adherence to a system that has been superseded by a new covenant under the Messiah. Moses was a magnificent servant of God, but he is dead. The Levitical priest has been replaced by a unique member of the tribe of Judah, not Levi!

As the writer of Hebrews said: with a change in the priesthood there is of necessity a change of the law, yes, a change of Torah! Jesus is our intercessor and High Priest at the right hand of the Father. It is not as though there are two names listed (Jesus and Moses) under heaven by which we can be saved. Just one! Our point is underlined by the fact that a new priest has risen:

"But a change of the priesthood must mean a change of law...For here is the testimony: 'You are a priest forever, in the order of Melchizedek.' *The earlier rules are repealed as ineffective and useless*, since the law brought nothing to perfection; and a better hope is introduced, through which we draw near to God" (Heb. 7:12-19).

The Cause of Spiritual Blindness

At the risk of belaboring the point, does not Paul warn us of spiritual blindness as a result of pursuing a Mosaic course of religious activity? We should note that the Jews, who are precise about keeping the laws of Moses, holy days, etc. are still in the dark about the Messiah who has come. This prevents them from being dedicated witnesses to the return of that same Christ to establish the Kingdom! Paul, passionate exponent of Judaism though he had been, certainly seemed unenthusiastic about the writings of Moses, if they prevented his audience from advancing to the Messiah: "In any case their minds have become closed, for that same veil is there to this very day when the lesson is read from the Old Covenant; and is never lifted, because *only* in Christ is it taken away. Indeed to this very day, every time the law of Moses is read, a veil is over the mind of the hearer. But (as scripture says) 'Whenever he turns to the Lord the veil is removed'" (2 Cor. 3:14-16).

Earlier verses in 2 Corinthians 3 thrill to the newness of spirit available under the New Covenant ministry of Jesus: "And as for you, it is plain that you are a letter that has come from Christ, given to us to deliver, a letter not written with ink but with the Spirit of the living God, written *not on stone tablets* but on the pages of the human heart" (3:3). The old covenant "ministry that brought death, and that was *engraved in written form on stone*" (3:7) is a shorthand description for the whole Mosaic system.

Sinai or Mt. Zion?

One is given a choice, either to accept the covenant made between God and ancient Israel under Moses and the Levitical priesthood, or the covenant between God and the present Israel of God under the Messiah. Paul talks of this in Galatians 6:15-16: "Circumcision is nothing;...the only thing that counts is a new creation. All who take this principle for their guide, peace and mercy be upon them, *the Israel of God*!" This covenant was made with Jesus and the priesthood of the order of Melchizedek.

Note the clearly stated contrast in Hebrews 12 between the New Covenant and the one made at Mt. Sinai. The writer starts his dissertation with the plain statement: "*It is not* to the tangible, blazing fire of Sinai that you [Christians] have come, with its darkness, gloom, and whirlwind, its trumpet blast and oracular voice, which the people heard and begged to hear no more; for they could not bear the command, 'If even an animal touches the mountain, it must be stoned to death.' So appalling was the sight that Moses said, 'I shudder with fear'" (12:18-21).

This is Mt. Sinai. This is where *you Christians have not come*, where the law was given under the Old Covenant that rules religious Israel to this very day. With this awesome exhibition God ushered in the Old Covenant. God's voice shook the very ground on which they stood. The covenant was inaugurated with a fearsome display of power. But Israel soon forgot.

But you Christians, have you come to Mt. Sinai for your instructions? "No, you have come to Mt. Zion, the city of the living God, the heavenly Jerusalem, to myriads of angels, to the full concourse and assembly of the firstborn who are enrolled in heaven, and to God the judge of all...and to Jesus the mediator of *a new covenant*...See that you do not refuse to hear the voice that speaks" (12:22-25).

Isn't this the echo of a long-ago admonition given by Moses to Israel in Deuteronomy 18:15: "The Lord your God will raise up for you a prophet like me from among your own people; it is to him *you must listen*"?

The writer of Hebrews does not leave us guessing at the implications of this scenario. He says, "By speaking of a new covenant, he has pronounced the *first one obsolete*; and anything that is becoming obsolete and growing old will shortly disappear" (Heb. 8:13). "The earlier rules are repealed as ineffective and useless, since the law brought nothing to perfection; and a better hope is introduced, through which we draw near to God" (7:18, 19). "But a change in the priesthood must mean a *change* of law" (7:12).

To sum up, we ask the question: Is Mt. Sinai where we find our home for laws and direction? The writer describes them as obsolete, growing old, shortly to disappear, ineffective, useless. This is Mt. Sinai! Paul comments on this same theme in his letter to the Galatians: "Tell me now, you that are so anxious to be under law, will you not listen to what the law says?...This is an allegory: the two women stand for two covenants. One covenant comes from Mt. Sinai; that is Hagar and her children born into slavery. Sinai is a mountain in Arabia and represents Jerusalem of today, for her children are in slavery [under the old Sinai covenant]. But the heavenly Jerusalem [Mt. Zion and the new covenant] is the free woman, she is our mother" (4:21-26).

One organization, in order to rescue their semi-Mosaic system, would have us believe that the expression "being under the law" means "being under the *penalty* of the law." No Scripture is quoted to support this concept. One could ask whether those whom Paul was addressing in this passage (Gal. 4:21) were people who were anxious to be *under the penalty of the* law? I would think not!

Which Days Do We Keep Unholy?

Paul writes about some persistent points of division and disagreement in the Christian church in Romans 14. His inspiration is "the law of concern" for fellow man. The issue is special days of worship and what we may or may not eat. On the question of varying opinions as to food he concludes, "Let us therefore cease judging one another, but rather make up our minds to place no stumbling block in a fellow Christian's way. All that I know of the Lord Jesus convinces me that **nothing is impure in itself**; only, if anyone considers something impure, then for him it is impure. If your fellow Christian is outraged by what you eat, then you are no longer guided by love. Do not let your eating be the ruin of one for whom Christ died. You must not let what you think good be brought into dispute; for the kingdom of God is not eating and drinking, but justice, peace and love, inspired by the Holy Sprit" (Rom. 14:13-17).

When Paul makes the statement in verse 20, "Do not destroy the work of God for the sake of food. *Everything is pure in itself*," one must assume that the writer's use of the word *everything* refers to food, not arsenic or barbed wire! In Paul's statement we find no support for enforcing Mosaic food laws. The Apostle recognized that a major problem is created if we require converts to Christ from the Gentile world to alter their diet by submitting to Moses. This would be to miss the point of the new international faith, "for the kingdom of God is not in eating and drinking, but justice, peace and joy inspired by the Holy Spirit" (Rom. 14:17).

Paul in Romans 14:14, 20 was certainly not affirming the food laws of Leviticus 11. In that chapter a precise list of animals, clean and unclean, is presented. To eat what is not prescribed is an abomination. Paul, however, in a chapter which mentions eating and food some 20 times, uses the *very opposite adjective* from the one found in Leviticus 11. There, under the law of Moses, foods are **clean** (*katharos*) or **unclean** (*akathartos*). For Paul, dealing expressly with eating and food, all things are *katharos* — **clean**. Curiously, Herbert Armstrong, in his booklet on this subject, stated the exact opposite in regard to Paul's language. Armstrong asserted that Paul had *not* used the opposite term from Leviticus 11.

Samuele Bacchiocchi evades the unwanted information by a similar misstatement of fact in regard to Paul's words: "That the Mosaic law is not at stake in Romans 14 is also indicated by the term 'koinos' — common, which is used in verse 14 to designate 'unclean' food. This term is radically different from the word 'akathartos' — impure, used in Leviticus 11 (LXX) to designate unlawful foods."[26]

What he does not tell us, however, is that Paul expressly reverses the Mosaic taboos when, *in verse 20*, he uses the *exact opposite* of "akathartos," unclean or impure, with his bold, liberating claim, "All things are pure." Paul here uses the term *katharos*, which is the opposite of *akathartos*. The Apostles had very clearly waived the temporary restrictions given to Israel under the law. For Paul the law (Torah) which alone has value is the "law of Christ" (Gal. 6:2; I Cor. 9:21), that is, the law as fulfilled in Christ, summed up as faith and love. Paul, after all, had written a whole book — Galatians — to explain that the law given to Israel through Moses was a temporary custodial guide valid only until the coming of Christ (Gal. 3:19-29). Paul was horrified that believers should want to move back under the Old Covenant, when Christ has

---

[26] *The Sabbath in the New Testament*, Biblical Perspectives, 1985, p. 134.

invited them to the freedom of the New Covenant brought by him as Messiah.

Hebrews 13:9 reinforces our lesson: "Do not be swept off your course by all sorts of outlandish teachings; it is good that we should gain inner strength from the grace of God, and not from rules about food which have never benefited those who have observed them." This statement points to the existence in the first century of Christians whose scruples over food were nothing but a burden to themselves and to others — and a potential cause of division and unrest in the church.

A leading commentary on Romans reads Paul with accuracy when it notes, "'Nothing is unclean of itself': This remarkable statement undercuts the whole distinction between clean and unclean foods on which Paul, like all other observant Jews, had been brought up."[27]

The same freedom of choice pertains to the selection of a day for worship: "Again, some make a distinction between this day and that; others regard all days alike. Everyone must act on his own convictions" (Rom. 14:5).

The Sabbath

When God the Creator and Father of mankind completed His six days of creation, He rested on the seventh day and declared it holy. It is not called the Sabbath but the "seventh day." The word *shabbat* is not used. To force the word *shabbat* on this particular seventh day adds to the text. There is no mention at this stage of a weekly Sabbath for mankind. No ordinance with a set of rules and regulations is given. Nor is there any scriptural support to show Sabbatical laws were imposed on Adam or his descendants until the time of the Exodus. That the Sabbath ordinance was mandated for all humanity is not

---

[27] John Ziezler, *Paul's Letter to the Romans*, p. 332.

stated in Genesis — a fact recognized by Jewish commentary.

The first seventh day has its own uniqueness. When the first six days are mentioned, each ends with the identifying phrase, "Evening came, and morning came." Then the particular day is noted. This is not the case with the seventh day on which God rested. There is no biblical record of any instruction given to Adam on how to conduct himself on subsequent seventh days. The word Sabbath appears nowhere in the Bible until Exodus 16:23 where, along with circumcision (Gen. 17:9-14), it becomes the divine *sign for Israel under the terms of the old Covenant* (Exod. 12:43-49).

Exodus 16:23: "Tomorrow is a Sabbath observance [not *the* Sabbath], a holy Sabbath to the Lord." 31:16, 17: "The Israelites must keep the Sabbath, observing it in every generation as a covenant *forever*. It is a *sign* forever between me and the Israelites, for in six days the Lord made the heavens and the earth, but on the seventh He ceased work and refreshed Himself." The Sabbath *originates* in this instruction through Moses (Neh. 9:13, 14; 10:29-33). The Sabbath was included in the summary of the law, the ten commandments: "When He finished speaking with Moses on Mt. Sinai, the Lord gave him two tablets of the Testimony, stone tablets written with the finger of God" (Exod. 31:18).

It should be noted that the word forever, *olam* in Hebrew, does not always contain the sense of permanence which it has for us. It is limited to a certain period of time, or as long as circumstances remain the same. The Sabbath finds its limitation as the sign along with circumcision in the Old Covenant, not the New Covenant. Physical circumcision was likewise commanded "forever" (Gen.

17:13, *olam*), but Christians in the New Testament did not insist on it.

The framework of obedience in which Christians must live is not that of the covenant given to Moses, Hebrews 12:18-29 speaks of New Covenant believers: We have *not come to Mt. Sinai.* 2 Corinthians 3:3-18 contrasts the killing effect of the letter of the law with the liberating power of the spirit. Blindness results from adherence to Moses. It is cured in Christ: "Whenever he turns to the Lord the veil is removed."

The Two Covenants

Psalm 110:4 says, "*God has sworn an oath* and will not change his mind, 'You are a priest forever, a Melchizedek in my service.'"

Repeated in Hebrews 7:17, this forms a crucial link between Jesus as a priest of the order of Melchizedek and the covenant with Abraham. This permitted the writer of Hebrews to assert categorically that the old priesthood and the law have been replaced by a new arrangement. "The Levitical priesthood and the law associated with it have been superseded by the new and 'better hope' based on the superior quality of the new priest...God announced His intention to set aside the whole Levitical system because it had proved to be ineffective in achieving its purpose. Its 'weakness' is not in the law or its purpose, but in the people upon whom it depends for its accomplishment. Its 'uselessness' derives from the fact that the law...was able to cleanse only externally."[28]

We appeal to Hebrews 7:28 for instructions on the difference between the two priesthoods: "The high priests appointed by law [the Levitical system] are men in all their weaknesses, but the priest appointed by *words of the oath*

---

[28] *Hebrews, Word Biblical Commentary*, p. 185.

which supersedes the law is the Son, who has been made perfect forever."

The writer of Hebrews shows the contrast between the new priesthood, whose appointment was validated by God's solemn oath, and the Levitical priesthood, which was based on the law *without the benefit of a divine oath*. This makes Jesus the priest of the new age. It states categorically that the new priesthood is a divine institution unconditionally guaranteed by God's solemn oath. The hopes of the Christian community are anchored in the absolute reliability of the New Covenant arrangements.

The promise to Abraham, the father of the faithful, was also confirmed by a divine oath (Heb. 6:13-18). This oath, not given to the Levitical priesthood, "is the impregnable guarantee that excludes all doubt and gives to faith assurance of the promise...It is final, eternal, and unchangeable."[29] This is not the case with the Levitical priesthood.

Entering God's Rest

We have noted the uniqueness of the seventh day of creation — the day of God's rest. This becomes a symbolic act for all humanity. It denotes a time when Christians cease from all our own work and its limited aims in our present mortal existence. God's rest points to a totally different set of goals and purposes by which to direct our lives. But it is not an effortless stroll towards a future position of authority promised in 1 Corinthians 6:2: "It is God's people who are to manage the world."

Israel under the Levitical priesthood sometimes kept the Sabbath, the holy days and new moons but too often strayed from the faith and obedience which would have led to the rest God designed for them. The writer of Hebrews

---

[29] *Ibid.,* p. 187.

provides the road back to success by quoting Psalm 95: "Today [this is for now!] if you hear his voice do not grow stubborn. If Joshua had given them rest, God would not have spoken of another day. Therefore, a Sabbath rest still awaits the people of God; anyone who enters God's rest, rests from his own work, as God did from His. Let us then make *every effort* to enter that rest, so that no one may fall by following the old example of unbelief" (Heb. 4:7-11).

We are not promised a relaxing walk in the park. We are, however, given the absolute assurance, the peace of mind and confidence that God has bound Himself, by an immutable oath through His Son, to carry us forward to the goal. How? By grasping our status as Hebrews 3:1-6 says: "Therefore, brothers of the family of God, partners in a heavenly calling, think of Jesus, the Apostle and High Priest of the faith we profess; he was faithful to God who appointed him...Jesus has been counted worthy of greater honor than Moses...*Christ is faithful as a son, set over the household. And we are that household, if only we are fearless* and keep our hope high."

The third and fourth chapters of Hebrews define the complete outline of what is required of us "now," "today," in order to enter the "rest" God offers. God is now working through His Son, the High Priest at His right hand. Success does not come through observing a semi-Mosaic system. We "have become partners with Christ if only we keep our initial confidence firm to the end" (3:14).

What does this partnership with God's risen Son entail? 4:1-3:"What we must fear therefore, is that, while the promise of entering his rest remains open, any one of you should be found to have missed his opportunity, for indeed we have had the good news preached to us, just as they had. But the message they heard did them no good, for it was not combined with faith in those who heard it.

Because we have faith, it is we who enter that rest." How then do we enter the rest which God designed for all humanity?

What is required is faith in the saving partnership with Jesus in proclaiming the Good News of a coming Kingdom of God on earth. Jesus said it was for this cause that his Father sent him. "I must give the good news of the kingdom of God to the other towns also, for that is what I was sent to do" (Luke 4:43). When Jesus carried out this task he entered into his "rest" by doing not his own work but the work of his Father. We can enter into that same "rest" and partnership with Jesus when we cease doing our *own* work and concentrate in collaboration with Jesus in doing God's work (Luke 4:43).

The field is the world. The seed is the Gospel message of the Kingdom (Matt. 13:19). In performing the work of sowing, Jesus assured his followers that they would one day occupy executive positions in the kingdom: "You have stayed with me through my trials; and just as my Father has covenanted to me the right to rule, so I covenant to you the same right. You will eat and drink at my table in my Kingdom, and you will sit on thrones to rule over the twelve tribes of Israel" (Luke 22:28-30). The task was to proclaim that Kingdom message to the world. The seed planted in the mind of peoples regardless of their circumstances did not demand adherence to the temporary laws of the Old Covenant, required for the discipline of the nation of Israel.

The change from Old Covenant requirements to the New Covenant is radical and dramatic. "Thou shalt not kill" is heightened to "love your enemies." And we are to set out on the ultimate quest for eternal life in the age to come: "Seek *first* the Kingdom of God and his righteousness" (Matt. 6:33).

The New Testament shifts to an emphasis on sharing the Gospel message of hope with anyone who will listen. It demands a love toward God the Creator and His Son Jesus who gave his life in sacrifice for our sins under a New Covenant. Jesus said, "If you love me keep my commandments." We enter rest (not a weekly Sabbath observance) by faith and obedience — a "sabbatism" (Heb. 4:9), not a single Sabbath day.

The writer of Hebrews is quite clear about the two different time frames. In chapters one and two he points to the exalted position given to Jesus now and in the age to come. Hebrews 2:5: "For it is not to angels that he has subjected the world to come [the coming New Age] which is our theme." And the subjection of this earth to man is yet future: "You put everything in subjection beneath his feet. For in subjecting everything to him, God left nothing that is made to be subject. But in fact we do *not yet* see everything in subjection to man" (2:8).

We are then invited to see in Chapter 3 the superiority of Jesus to Moses and that "today [now] if you will hear his [Jesus'] voice" we become partners with him (not Moses). The New Covenant is not a mixture of the Old Covenant and the New. Paul sweeps away the Old Covenant and its relevance for today when he says in Colossians 2:9-17: "For it is in Christ the Godhead in all its fullness dwells embodied; it is in him you have been brought to fulfillment. Every power and authority in the universe is subject to him as head. In him you were circumcised, *not in a physical sense*, but by stripping away of the old nature, which is Christ's way of circumcision…And although you were dead because of your sins…he has brought you to life with Christ. For he has forgiven us all our sins: he has cancelled the bond which was outstanding against us with its legal demands; he has set it aside, nailing it to the cross...

"Therefore, allow no one to take you to task about what you eat or drink, or over the observance of a festival, new moon, or sabbath. These are no more than a shadow of what was to come; the reality is Christ's."

With this "trio" of Jewish sacred days Paul refers to a unit of observances to which Christians are *not* to feel obligated. No less than 11 times in the Old Testament this description of the weekly, monthly and annual observances appears as *one* package. Paul sees all three as a *single* shadow. Sabbaths — annual, monthly and weekly — are plainly and equally "types" of the one who is our Passover, our Sabbath and our Atonement, our rest. Moses is dead. Christ lives!

This is what I see as a fundamental issue: God gave us through His Son a commission to bring a message of hope to the entire world. We are invited to join His Son in *that* commission. Mosaic barriers to getting that message to the world have been eliminated. We are now free to move around the world. I may well be in Malawi during the days of Unleavened Bread. Breadcrumbs in the houses will not be an issue. They will be lucky to have had any bread to produce crumbs!

It is an enormous blessing to possess the knowledge of the unique God of Israel. The same belief is held by millions of Jews. Over a billion Muslims also believe there is One God. Unfortunately for the Jews they look to Moses. They have rejected the Messiah who came. The Muslims look to Mohammed. Some believers in Jesus still look partly to Moses and not fully to the Messiah who came not to abolish the Torah but to *complete it*. Paul insists that compromising the Old with the New is a way to blindness. 2 Corinthians 3:14-16: "In any case their minds had become closed. For to this day, when they read the old covenant, that same veil remains unlifted, because only through Christ is it taken away. Yes, to this day whenever Moses is read a veil lies over their hearts. But when one turns to the Lord, the veil is removed."

Letter to a Friend

The following is an extract from a letter written by Mrs. Lynn Gray to a friend and fellow ex-member of the Worldwide Church of God. Mrs. Gray has expressed with simple clarity her excitement at finding freedom in the spirit of the New Covenant (the name of the addressee has been changed).

"When you were here we were discussing Colossians 2:16, 17. You felt Paul meant that Christians in Colosse were being persecuted for not keeping the holy days in the legalistic manner of the Pharisees. How do you reach that conclusion when Paul said those days themselves were shadows and we are no longer to be in the shadow? The way you are reading it is contradictory. I always felt this was contradictory when I was in the Worldwide Church of God. Their explanation never made a bit of sense. I did accept their explanation because I thought 'the Apostle' knew all. I think the context here in Colossians is very plain. Paul is saying that those days are no longer binding in a literal way as they were under the Old Covenant. It was not just the Talmudic point by point legalism that was in question. It was the Old Covenant itself. The picky legalism, like how far a person could walk on the Sabbath, and all the other hundreds of do's and don'ts, were mostly added down through the centuries of Jewish tradition. This is man's law, not God's, and was never necessary. It was a running commentary of legislation added to the Old Covenant. But this is not what Paul refers to as a shadow. It is the Old Covenant itself. The Jewish additions to the

Bible never had any status even as shadows. For Paul the do's and don'ts go out of the window with the Old Covenant legal system.

"In many other Scriptures, Paul says he was not under the law: that he became as a Jew to win the Jews. Apparently he no longer considered himself a Jew. He is referring to much more than legalism and the penalty of the law in these verses. To say that we should still keep those days minus the legalism totally misses the point. Christ's deliverance from the Old Covenant was a lot more than deliverance from Jewish legalism.

"I loved those days and observances at one time. I loved the holy days and the Sabbath just as you do now. (The holy days became much more of a burden when I went to work.) At the same time as I loved them I also lived in fear that I would somehow do something wrong and sinful on those days. But Jane, I viewed those days as holy, sacred and wonderful. What you don't understand is that there is something better. The New Covenant which does not consist of the letter of the law. It is a better way. It is a much more loving way. It affords the opportunity to draw even closer to Christ and God. It is much more wonderful than keeping the Sabbath and holy days. Believe me, Jane, this way is better. Much, much better. Until you come out from the shadow you will limit Christ in your life. There is a love when one is not in the shadow which you can only experience when you come out of the shadow. To keep the old law is to hinder one's relationship with Christ. It makes his life and death far less significant when we fail to realize the liberty and freedom that he brought us. Jane, I really believe you are the one missing out on the love that is there. But that is something that we all have to find in our own time and space. It certainly has taken me a while...

"Also one more point. I do not believe that because Paul went to the synagogue on the Sabbath that this is proof that he kept the Sabbath. It is clear that he would have to go into the synagogues on the Sabbath if he wanted to reach his brethren with the Gospel. That makes perfect sense to me. There is no proof that Paul kept the holy days, etc., except as a way of making contact with fellow Jews. In fact there is ample proof that these things were no longer important to him and that he taught others about liberty in Christ.

"It takes study and understanding and the holy spirit to grasp the difference between the Old Covenant and the New. If we are to be Christians as Paul and others were we must come out of the shadows — and rest in Christ, every day."